STO

The Stronghold

Also by Mollie Hunter

THE WALKING STONES
THE THIRTEENTH MEMBER
THE HAUNTED MOUNTAIN
A SOUND OF CHARIOTS

Harper & Row, Publishers
New York   Evanston   San Francisco   London

The Stronghold

by Mollie Hunter

With love to my gentle Bronwen, who gave me Fand.

M.H.

1798803

Table of Contents

Foreword

Ten years ago I stood inside one of the massive stone structures which are known to archaeologists as "brochs." I wondered how it had come to be built, why, and when; and this book was born.

Brochs can only be found in the north of Scotland and on the islands off Scotland's northern coast, and it was on the island group called the Orkney Islands that they are thought to have originated. More than five hundred of them exist, all situated on or near arable land, and all close to the sea. Their structure is purely defensive. Their siting indicates that this defense was intended against danger from the sea. The conjecture is, therefore, that this seaborne danger came from the Roman Navy, which is known to have been raiding for slaves from these northern coasts during the time the brochs were built—a period dating from about the middle of the first century B.C. to the end of the first century A.D.

A further fact about the brochs is that they all conform to a uniform design; which fact, together with the feat of building five hundred structures of such size and strength over this comparatively short period, argues that teams of professional builders were involved either in instructing, or in helping with the work. The most striking of all the facts about the brochs, however, is that the design they follow is unique. It has no parallel and no precedent anywhere else in the world. *It must therefore have been an idea before it was a fact; an idea springing from one single brilliant mind.*

Who was this unnamed genius? I wish I knew. But even although that can never be, I felt something of the power of his mind that day inside the broch; and in THE STRONGHOLD, I have told his story as I think it might have happened.

Mollie Hunter

1
Confrontation

They came from inland of the ridge behind the settlement in the bay, and streamed swiftly down to the fortress of Nectan, their Chief. They came from the seaward side of the settlement also, in small boats of sealskin stretched taut over narrow whalebone frames; warriors, bearing the mark of the Boar on their foreheads, leaping ashore to meet the other warriors streaming toward Nectan's *dun*.

The two streams converged, bronze-decorated shields gleaming in the sun of the late-autumn day, long iron-bladed spears thrusting a wicked hedge of points above the shields. And gazing down from the headland guarding the northwest aspect of the bay, Coll felt all the urgency of his eighteen years impelling him to join this muster of his fellow tribesmen.

But he was on lookout duty, he reminded himself. It was his turn that morning to watch for the Roman slave raiders who were the cause of the muster, and not even Nectan's foster son could be excused a moment of that duty. He could leave once Drostan, his relief man, arrived; and not until then.

Reluctantly Coll turned his gaze away from the settlement, and once more braced his sinewy frame to meet the cold sea wind whistling over the headland. The movement woke pain in his crippled leg, and he endured it with gritted teeth and a tightened grip on the long stem of the bronze warning trumpet in his right hand. The pain passed. His fingers relaxed, and his face regained its normal appearance of spare, bony strength.

Watchfully then, he faced south to the sea again; for it was from the south the raiders always struck—from the long arm of sea stretching out toward the turbulent tidal race that separated the Orkney Islands from the mainland of North Britain. And it was his own island—the largest by far among the scores in the territory of Ork, the Boar—that had suffered most from their attacks.

With eyes narrowed, and a steady stance that ignored the wind making long streamers of his hair and whipping his tunic around his knees, Coll kept his gaze on the blue, rippled water six hundred feet below; and did not turn again from the last intent hour of his watch until Drostan had climbed the last few feet of the headland to stand beside him.

"Not a stranger craft in sight all morning!"

Coll handed the warning trumpet over to Drostan as he spoke, and glancing down to the figures swarming about the settlement on the shoreline of the bay, he added,

"And it looks as if the other settlements have sent every man they could to the muster."

"Close on seven hundred," Drostan told him cheerfully, and Coll's glance roved farther, searching on the outskirts of the muster for the white robes of Domnall, the Chief of the islands' priesthood of Druids. Drostan guessed at the reason for his searching look, and told him, "Look over there, and you will see Domnall coming."

Coll followed the finger pointing him toward the treeless and smoothly rounded contours of the island's landward aspect, and caught a glimpse of something white moving toward the bay.

"I see him," he told Drostan. "But, by the gods, I wish otherwise, for Nectan is a stubborn man. He will hold to his decision about the raiders, however hard he may clash with Domnall."

A grin split Drostan's cheerful face. "Nectan will not be the loser in this clash," he predicted confidently. Then, with a look that envied Coll, he added, "I only wish *I* could be there to hear him dispute with Domnall."

Coll nodded his sympathy. "But keep a good watch all the same," he warned, and turned to hurry away down the headland.

It was a sharp descent to the bay, and rough going for him over the turf that only thinly concealed the stony surface of the slope. For all his eagerness to reach the settlement, Coll found himself wincing from one jarring impact after another on his lame leg, and an old memory began to darken his mind. . . .

He was five years old and he was screaming in terror at his first sight of the raiders leaping ashore to the beach below the headland. . . . He was running from them, blundering away from the place where the dead and bloody body of his father lay. He saw his mother, and reached out to grasp the illusion of safety in her. A hand wrenched the stuff of her dress from his grip. Another hand plucked strongly at his hair. He was swung upward by the hair until his face was level with that of the man holding him. He clawed the air, his screams rising to a dementia of terror at the nearness of the face under the great shining orb of its Roman helmet. The hand entwined in his hair swung him contemptuously into space. The rocks of the beach came spinning toward him. There was pain—violent sickening pain as he came crashing down against the rocks. . . .

With a muttered exclamation, Coll stopped to wipe away the sweat that had broken out on his forehead, then fiercely he massaged the hipbone which had been broken in his fall and which had set so badly. It was the nightmare again, the recurrent daytime nightmare left like a curse with him from the raid that had crippled him like this!

But he would banish that nightmare yet, he vowed. Some day, when he had found the answer to his scheme for building a Stronghold against the attacks of the raiders. Some day, when he had provided the whole tribe with a perfect defense against them!

He glanced seaward, half expecting to see the raiders' boats shooting black and huge again out of the sun's eye, but the sea was still an empty blue calm. His glance came back to the bay, and he saw that the tribesmen were now massed around the Stone of the Crowning outside Nectan's dun, with an open space in their ranks to allow Domnall to approach the Stone.

Hastily he continued to the foot of the slope and broke into a limping run through the settlement's scatter of houses, each with its complement of women and children grouped in patient and watchful silence at its doorway. The freemen of the tribe—those who had a skill to follow when not engaged in such a call to arms—formed the outer ranks of the gathering around the Stone of the Crowning. Quickly he worked his way through them to the aristocratic heart of the crowd—the warrior captains lined on either side of the Stone.

They made way for him, although he was not of their number, recognizing the position due to him as Nectan's foster son, and he chose a stance that was only a few feet away from the flat bulk of the Stone. Almost immediately, then, his eye caught that of Nectan's younger daughter, Fand.

She was standing with her sister Clodha and her mother Anu, in the place of honor at Nectan's right side, and her slight figure looked fragile beside the tall and sturdy build of the other two. She was paler than usual too, Coll noticed, and thought how young and vulnerable she looked in such a setting. He smiled reassuringly at her, and waited for her nervous answering smile before glancing at Nectan himself.

The Chief of the Boar stood very erect, and plainly determined that the battle with Domnall would indeed be a stiff one. His feet were firmly planted in the two shallow foot-shaped hollows in the Stone where, twenty years before, they had been placed to have the sacred shoes of a ruler put on them. The muscles of his powerful frame were flexed. The blue tattoo mark of the wild boar seemed more than ordinarily bright on his forehead, and his face was scowling under the weight of the gold-mounted boar's skull that crowned him.

Or was he scowling at the sight of Domnall? Coll's gaze followed that of Nectan until it encountered a white-robed figure moving slow and stately through the ranks of the tribe's warrior aristocracy. His heart seemed to skip a beat then, and a strong sense of unease gripped him; for Domnall was also grim-faced, and at that moment it was hard to judge between the apparent authority of the two men. Instinctively, Coll compared one with the other.

Nectan was splendid in his strength—and that counted for much among a people who admired physical power. He looked magnificently the part of a Chief, too, with the gold-snarling boar's skull crowning him, the golden torque that coiled like a snake around his neck, and the breast of his tunic ornamented by a great sunburst of gold.

But Domnall was also a man of great strength, and he wore the simple robes of his priesthood with an air of massive dignity. Moreover, his gray beard proclaimed his advantage of twenty years' experience over Nectan. And quite apart from that, Domnall had strange powers at his command—magical powers that came straight from the gods themselves. . . .

Coll found himself remembering the many times he had been part of an identical gathering of the Boar watching in tense silence as Domnall led the whole Druid priesthood of the islands in the sacrifice ritual demanded by the Otherworld gods. A familiar awe gripped him, and with it came a sweat of panic at the risk Nectan was taking.

What if Domnall was so angered by this confrontation that he turned against them all? What would they do then? How could they live without the Druid ceremonies to protect them from those dreaded powers of the Otherworld?

With his uneasiness grown to a positive foreboding of disaster, Coll watched the Chief Druid halt a few feet away from Nectan. The two men confronted one another in silence for a moment, then Nectan opened his mouth to speak. But swiftly, ruthlessly, Domnall robbed him of the first strike in the battle, his voice rolling strongly out for all the tribe to hear.

"Shall any man, even a Chief, speak before his Druid speaks?"

It was the law—Domnall did have the right to speak first! Nectan bit his lip in anger at the unanswerable challenge of the question. The Druid's glance measured him, marking the effect of this first small victory gained. Then, turning from him, he raised his arms high, and let the rich strong tones of his voice roll out again.

"Hear me, Men of the Boar. Hear your Druid! It has come to my ears that Nectan has decided you will no longer stand and fight against the Romans who raid your islands for slaves. That does not please me! And that is why I sent to tell him I would appear today before you all to challenge that decision."

"Hold, Domnall!" Raspingly, his anger still plain to see, Nectan interrupted. "The people have not yet had opportunity to know the reason for my decision. Let them hear that now, before you condemn it."

There was a ripple of movement in the Council of Elders grouped behind Nectan. Heads nodded, voices murmured support for his protest; and with a swift glance that assessed the degree of this support, Domnall altered his tactics to suit it. Graciously, with a gesture that invited Nectan to continue, he announced,

"It is their right."

Nectan looked out over the throng of watching faces. "Hear me, then," he shouted. "Hear your Chief! We make a brave show of strength, gathered here today from every island of Ork the Boar—but this is not how the raiders find us! We need the fertile coastlands to cultivate, and the sea to harvest; and so it is our way to live in small and scattered settlements of no more than a few hundred people. For all our fighting spirit, therefore, the raiders find us an easy mark, and our tribe grows weak from the struggle against them.

"We grow too weak, Men of the Boar! Too many of our warriors are killed in battle with the raiders. Too many of our young people are captured into slavery. Thus, in time, we shall fall prey also to our other enemies, the inland tribes of the Raven and the Deer. And so I have met in Council with your elected Elders, and we have come to this agreement. When a settlement is attacked by the raiders, we shall no longer put up a brave and uselessly bloody resistance. Instead, you warriors will scatter, taking the women and children with you, until the raiders have gone and it is safe for everyone to return to their homes."

"No!" Violently Domnall shouted the word. "The power of Rome must be resisted wherever it appears!"

"And I say we have done our share in that!"

With a shout as violent, Nectan answered the Druid, and passionately continued, "Every one of our settlements has fought the raiders in turn. And when our losses grew too high from such lone engagements, we

8

posted lookouts that would bring as many more warriors as possible to the help of those attacked. Yet what has been the result of all this?"

Fiercely Nectan flung out a pointing hand, and fiercely he urged, "Look, Domnall! Look at these men who carry the mark of the Boar on their foreheads, and see how their numbers have become fewer over the years. Count the graves on the ridge behind you there, and the warriors lying in them. And look here! See the age now of some who wear the golden torque of a captain of warriors around their necks!"

Swinging about on the words, he caught the arm of the warrior standing behind his elder daughter, Clodha, and pulled him forward.

"Here!" he told Domnall angrily. "Here is Niall, son of Oengus, and he is but eighteen years old. Yet this is the kind of young blood I now have to allow into the Council—and all for lack of men whose years would make them fitter to be elected."

"Or perhaps it is because you think it wise to have Clodha's intended husband under your eye there!"

Swift and skillfully Domnall planted the barb of his suggestion, and with dismay, Coll saw how Nectan had blundered; for it was true that he looked favorably on Niall's courtship of Clodha. It was true also that it suited him to have Niall on the Council where he could be molded to Nectan's own way of thinking; for succession in the tribe came through the female line, and when Niall married Clodha, it was Niall who would become Chief in Nectan's place.

And there were others, Coll realized, who were aware that Nectan had made a mistake in bringing Niall forward to prove his point. The older members of the Council were frowning their disapproval of the blunder; and as for the rest of the tribespeople, it had begun to look as if they were uneasy over the violence of Nectan's opposition to the Chief Druid. There was fear on many of the faces in the crowd—indeed, Coll thought, he could feel a shiver of that fear himself! And was not surprised when Domnall followed quickly on the advantage gained.

"Is this all the case, then, that Nectan can put for you? That many of you have died fighting the raiders, and many more may do so. Are you so afraid of them, Men of the Boar?"

Contemptuously he flung his last question at the crowd, and raised his voice powerfully over the angry mutter of dissent it provoked.

"For if you are afraid, you deserve the opinion the Romans hold of all those they call barbarians. You are indeed only fit to be part of the great slave mass that supports the power of Rome. And the Romans' war leader was right when he said that slaves would be the chief prize to be gained from the conquest of Britain and its islands!"

Domnall paused, shrewdly assessing the faces before him for the effect of these jibes. Then, pointing southward to the unseen mainland of Britain, he shouted,

"But Rome is not all-powerful, Men of the Boar, for that same Caesar who leads the legions has twice brought them to attack the southern tribes of the mainland there, and twice he has been driven away. Therefore I tell you that the power of Rome *can* be resisted. It *must* be resisted, whenever or however it appears, for only then will the Romans learn that they cannot sweep like conquerors over any land they choose to invade!"

"We are in no danger of invasion!"

It was Nectan, loudly challenging again, determinedly trying to recover lost ground. But Domnall was in the full flood of his argument now, and promptly he retorted,

"How can you tell that? The Romans are content, meantime, to raid thus far afield for slaves; but the day will come when they need an easier source of supply, and it is certain then that they will make another attempt to conquer the mainland. Do you suppose, if they succeed in this, they will leave *you* at peace in your islands?"

"That day, if it ever comes, is still far ahead," Nectan persisted stubbornly. "And meanwhile, it is my duty as Chief to protect the people of the Boar, and to rule them for their own good."

"Your first duty," Domnall snapped, "is to obey me in matters of faith!"

"And have I not always done that?" Hot resentment flushing in his face, Nectan challenged the Druid, and grimly Domnall told him,

"Then learn this, Nectan, for I tell it to you now for your own good. Resistance to Rome has been declared a matter of faith among all peoples who have Druids for their priests; and you will obey that ruling also, or suffer the consequences!"

Quickly, before Nectan could reply to this, Domnall turned from him and shouted, "You have all heard this defiance of me, and so now hear also what will happen to Nectan if he disobeys my command to stand and fight against the Roman raiders. I am your Druid! I have powers that are denied to other men, and I shall use these powers to lay a curse on Nectan! Hear this, Men of the Boar, and be warned. Hear this, and fear your Druid!"

Domnall's voice had reached the peak of its power now. Like a trumpet blast sounding forth, the words of his threat rang out across the empty vastness of the sea around the islands, soared into the blue emptiness of sky arching over them. And as the last vibrating note of it died away, it was answered by another trumpet note; faint and far away, but still clearly sounding forth.

As one head turning, then, the heads of all present turned to this second sound—the warning trumpet call of the lookout at the summit of the headland. Time ceased in a long frozen moment of inaction; then Nectan's voice roaring out the command for battle stations shattered the timeless moment.

"*The raiders!*" In spite of the wild leap of terror his heart always gave at the impact of this thought, Coll spared a quick glance for Fand before he ran for his own battle position. The guards appointed for the protection of Nectan's womenfolk were hustling her and Clodha and Anu off as usual to the underground hiding place Nectan had prepared for them, and immediately he saw this, Coll forgot about everything except the need to move quickly to his station.

In a flurry of sand and pebbles spurting from under his feet, he covered the part of the beach that lay between himself and the fire pit. The fire was lit there—it was always kept burning and needed only to be blown furiously into flaring life. The stack of dry peat to feed the blaze was ready beside it, and sheltered under the same covering of skins were the fire spears with their shafts dipped in seal oil and their heads bound with dried peat fibers.

With carefully rapid movements Coll conjured the needed blaze from the fire pit and fed the hungry flames. This was the tribe's first line of defense—the hail of blazing spears that could succeed in setting the timbers of the raiders' boats alight, and so force them to choose between drawing off or losing their boats to the flames. And then—!

Stealing sidelong glances past the waiting spearmen lined up by his fire pit as he worked, Coll saw other spearmen fanning along the rocks to find vantage points for thrusting at the raiders as they waded ashore.

The slingsmen were filling their pouches from the supply of stones on the beach. Nectan had taken his swordsmen across the wide ditch below the great stone wall encircling his dun, and now they were manning these final two lines of defense.

If the fire spears failed this time, Coll thought exultantly, there was still no doubt that they could beat the raiders off. For this time—thanks to the visit of Domnall—they had all the Men of the Boar gathered at one point instead of being scattered over the tribe's various settlements!

He spared time for a longer glance around and saw some of the women and children still running to hide among the tumble of big rocks at the foot of the headland. Then, suddenly, he glimpsed the white of Domnall's robe among the swordsmen on the wall around Nectan's dun and heard Domnall's voice raised in the ritual cursing of the enemy before battle.

His skin prickled at the sound, and he felt the surging of a wild impulse to lift his head and howl in concert with the howling figure poised aloft on the wall. The rise and fall of Domnall's voice rang through him as if his body

had become a sounding board for its vibrations—
Domnall shouting that the gods loved courage in battle
above all things, Domnall shrieking vengeance on the
enemies of the gods, Domnall howling the battle cry of
the Men of the Boar. . . .

Coll straightened up, a spear with a blazing point
gripped in one hand, a bubble of sound rising in his
throat. The bubble broke and became a moaning noise
that grew and grew in volume. His head jerked back, his
mouth opened wide, and the moan became the long,
howling notes of his tribe's battle cry. Then somehow he
found he was stamping about on the shingle, brandishing
the blazing spear above his head; and suddenly he was no
longer Coll the cripple. He was Coll of the tribe of the
Boar, with a fierce and ancient anger firing his brain—
Coll the warrior with a scarlet spear raised high—Coll
the Boar, the wild boar roaring and stamping his anger
before he charged his enemies. . . .

Drostan, the lookout man who had blown the warning
trumpet, found the whole fighting force of the tribe
caught up in the same frenzy when he came running
down from his position on the headland; and the message
he had brought fell at first on deaf ears. Impatiently
pushing stamping, howling warriors aside, he reached
Nectan and shouted once more,

*"There is no need to prepare for battle! The raiders
are not here!"*

Nectan was arrested in mid-gesture, the fierce joy in
his face changing swiftly to a murderous anger.

"So you sounded a false alarm!" he roared, and lunged
with outspread hands closing vengefully around Drostan's throat.

14

It was the young warrior, Niall, who saved Drostan's life then, tearing at Nectan's hands and loudly protesting,

"Give him time to talk, Nectan! Give him time! He must have had *some* reason for sounding the warning!"

Nectan's grip slackened. Reluctantly he dropped his hands and stepped back; and gulping a breath of air, Drostan hurried to tell him,

"I sighted a boat—only a small one, but the man in it was not one of our people. I could see that by the shape of the boat itself, and I thought it might be a scout—a spy—for the Men of the Raven, or the Deer. I had no way of telling, and so I *had* to sound the alarm."

"Where is he, then? Show him to me! He must be in sight by now." Nectan took a grip on Drostan's shoulder, and angrily repeating, "Show him to me!" began propelling him toward the beach.

They stumbled together over the shingle, and word of Drostan's news spread as they went. The slingsmen and spearmen crowded behind them and, one after another, began to point to the boat heading in from the bay. Drostan pointed also, sullenly indicating it to Nectan.

"Out there! There is the boat I saw."

It was a little boat, almost round in shape and with room for only one man in it. Coll edged into the crowd watching it skim shoreward and saw for himself what had alarmed Drostan, for this boat's shape was certainly most unlike any of their own narrow and sharp-prowed craft.

"Bring him to me when he beaches," Nectan ordered, and impatiently pushed his way back to the Stone of the Crowning.

From the corner of his eye Coll saw Domnall move toward the same place. A strangely empty feeling replaced the excitement he had felt, and slowly he moved to join the tribesmen who were also drifting back to the Stone. Silently sharing their suspicions of the man in the little boat, he watched it drawing nearer and nearer to the beach.

The men who had stayed at the water's edge laid hold of it the moment it beached. Some of them steadied it, others hauled the rower bodily from it. He was a man in the prime of youthful strength, yet even so he made no effort to resist this rude handling; and within seconds of being seized, he was being hustled up the beach to stand in front of Nectan.

"Loose him," Nectan ordered, and the tribesmen dropped their hold of the stranger.

Nectan studied him in silent distaste for a moment, for the man wore nothing except a strip of cloth around his loins; and such nakedness, apart from the ritual nakedness of a warrior in battle, was an offense against the gods. The man did not flinch under this look, and harshly Nectan ordered,

"Tell me your tribe, stranger. And by your life, answer me truly."

"I will give you true answer."

The strange man spoke slowly, raising one hand to his brow as he did so. He brushed aside the lock of hair hiding his forehead, and Nectan saw the design of a wild boar tattooed blue on the skin there.

"This is my tribe—your tribe; the tribe of the Boar," the stranger told Nectan. Then calmly he turned his head right and left so that everyone near him could see the mark of the Boar on his forehead.

"And your name?" The question came from Nectan in

a voice that was husky with astonishment, but the stranger made no immediate answer. He was looking around the gathering of tribesmen now, his eyes taking in the spears, the swords, the pouches heavy with sling shot. His gaze passed beyond them to where Coll's supply of spears lay ready on the beach beside the smoking fire pit, and then came finally back to rest on Nectan again.

"You were expecting a raid." It was a statement, not a question, and Nectan nodded in reply.

"But not from another tribe," he added. "It was Roman slave raiders we were prepared to fight."

The young man smiled, a twisted sort of smile that gave a cruel cast to his features. "My name is Taran," he said, "and I was a boy of twelve when these same raiders captured me from this tribe. They took me south to the land of Gaul, and sold me into slavery there. But I come of noble stock, of the line of Keridwen, which has always mated with warriors, and bred warriors—"

"Now I know you!" Nectan interrupted. "I remember that raid! It was the one that happened thirteen years ago, when so many of the women were killed—your mother, Birgit, among them. And I remember we thought the name of Keridwen was dead with your mother, for you and she were the last of that line!"

"But now you see me again." Taran, of the line of Keridwen, spoke with a look of grim triumph replacing his cruel little smile. "Now you see how wrong you were, for I swore by that same warrior blood to break free of my Roman master and, however hard and dangerous the journey might be, to make my way back to the land of the Boar."

"How *did* you break free of your Roman master?"

It was Domnall who spoke into the little silence that followed this speech, and Taran looked surprised at his question.

"I killed him, of course," he answered. "What else should I have done?"

Domnall studied the surprised face, veined eyelids screening the look of speculation in his own eyes, raised eyebrows wrinkling his forehead into a high, questioning arch.

"Of course," he agreed. "What else!"

There was irony in the Druid's voice, but Taran seemed unaware of this. Drawing himself erect, he launched proudly into the full account of his lineage that custom required before he could finally be accepted as a warrior among the warriors of the Boar. And with all eyes focusing attention on this, Domnall was free to make his own assessment of the man who claimed to have such a ruthless way with the hated Roman.

2
Taran

At the southeast end of the bay, where great slabs of red sandstone lay piled on the beach, Coll was patiently building yet another model for the structure he thought of as his Stronghold.

Clodha and Niall sat together on a recumbent slab of the reddish-brown rock, a study in contrasting good looks, with Clodha as dark as Niall was fair. Fand crouched at their feet, soft brown hair swinging over her face, blue eyes intent on a pebble she had picked up and was polishing vigorously to brightness.

It was a day in early spring. Thin sunshine gilded the first faint green that hazed the low-lying contours of the islands. A million points of light trembled on the surrounding seas. From a distant view, the golden-green haze seemed to float on the sparkling blue like a shimmering dream of islands; but on the land itself, reality wore a harsher, bleaker face.

The day was a cold one. The wind that blew so often over the islands had a knife-sharp edge. Coll found himself thinking that the winter which had followed Nectan's confrontation with Domnall had seemed a very long one; and with a glance at the slender forms of the two girls huddled into the fur of their cloaks, he wondered when they would have some sunshine with real warmth in it. His glance traveled to Niall's face, noting the preoccupied frown it wore, and his busy hands paused as Clodha asked,

"Well, Niall?"

"Well, Clodha?" Niall mimicked her with a sour note in his normally good-humored voice. "You know why I wanted you all here in our private meeting place. Nectan has passed a whole winter without giving any sign of his intentions, and it is time we knew what they are. Does he mean to yield to Domnall's threat? Or will he call another meeting of the Council to confirm the policy of dispersing before the attacks of the slave raiders?"

Clodha glanced seaward. "The raiding ships will not come until the summer," she reminded Niall. "They never do. And perhaps they will not come at all this year. They do not come every year, after all."

"That would be no answer to the problem," Niall retorted. "Domnall will want to know *this* year whether or not Nectan means to obey him."

"If Nectan disobeys," Coll remarked, "he will be the only island Chief to do so. The Men of the Raven have promised to resist the slavers—the Men of the Deer also."

"An empty promise from inland tribes in little danger from such raids," Niall told him scornfully. "But we of the Boar, who have our settlements on the coast—we take the brunt of the attacks."

"There is something else to consider," Clodha pointed

out. "The Deer and the Raven hate us for our command of the sea and the fertile coastlands, and if we scatter before the raiders these tribes could combine to make us prey to *their* attacks."

"Not so," Niall contradicted. "Raven and Deer have always been disunited. Moreover, their settlements are smaller than ours, and their men poorly armed. We could deal easily with them, as we always have in the past. But how long do you think we can survive as the ruling tribe of the islands when so many of our warriors fall to the raiders? How long can we survive at all when so many of our children and young people are captured by them?"

Rising from his place on the rock, he began pacing restlessly up and down, and stopped at last in front of Clodha.

"When you and I marry," he reminded her, "I shall have the responsibility of succeeding to Nectan's position; and so I have a greater stake than anyone on the outcome of his decisions. Yet he will not speak to me or to anyone about what he intends, and *someone* must break through that barrier of silence for me—you, Clodha. You must discover what he means to do."

Clodha shook her head. "Does a daughter have more privilege than a wife?" she asked. "Nectan will not even tell Anu what is in his mind now, and so why should he speak to me?"

Niall looked at Fand. "You are his favorite—his pet," he told her. "Can you not coax him out of this sullen silence?"

"I might," Fand admitted uneasily. "But to what point, Niall? Nectan would never dream of discussing such matters with me."

"Then I shall challenge him myself," Niall declared. "And I shall tell him that if he does call another meeting of the Council, I for one shall vote that we keep to our first decision about the raiders."

"But what of Domnall's curse?" Fand asked. She glanced up at Niall with an apprehension that made her look suddenly younger than her fifteen years, and added fearfully, "Do you want it to fall on all of us?"

"That will not happen unless we all oppose Domnall," Clodha assured her. "But you need not fear such a state of affairs, for some at least of the Councillors would be afraid to risk it."

Fand sighed in relief, but Niall gave an angry shake of his blond head. "And so," he said violently, "the tribe will be divided, and we shall be in even worse case than ever to deal with the raiders."

No one answered this, and it was Coll who eventually broke the silence that fell. "You all talk as if there were only two choices open to us," he said reprovingly, "to follow Nectan's way or Domnall's way. Have you forgotten that my Stronghold would provide a third choice, one that would satisfy both Domnall and Nectan? If I could—"

"If—!" Niall interrupted. "If—! Coll, you have been talking like that since we were both little boys of five. But you never finish any of those towers you make. You build a bit of wall here, a bit there—"

"And with good reason!" Sharply Coll stemmed the threatened tirade. "It is a long time since I was a frightened little boy trying desperately to invent some kind of safe place where I could hide from the raiders; and every one of those unfinished towers has taught me *something* of the purpose that developed from my fear. You know that, Niall. You know that what I am trying to do is to create a system of defense against the raiders—a perfect defense that we can hold against all their attacks. And now I think I am almost on the point of understanding how to create that defense."

With a wave of his arm, Coll indicated the settlement. "Look along there, Niall," he urged, "and tell me what you see about the building methods of the people of the Boar."

Niall turned to stare toward the scatter of small, bee-hive-shaped dwellings, made even smaller by distance and by their proximity to the great circular shape of Nectan's dun with its arching roof of reed-thatched whale-bone.

"I see that we build always in stone," he told Coll impatiently, "but that is because the sandstone of the beaches gives a good supply of material ready to hand. I see that we are very skillful at fitting one stone upon another, without the need of any binding substance. And we build always in the shape of a circle, because we know that a circle has no one point that is weaker than another—but indeed, a bird knows as much when it builds its nest!"

A grin flashed across Coll's angular features—a rare event for one of his serious nature. "And so," he capped Niall's remarks, "I know that I could build a tower to a shape which would give its walls an even strength, and which—because it would be of stone—could not even be overcome by fire. But you have forgotten to mention, Niall, that none of our present buildings is more than the head height of a man—all due to the fact that we live on treeless islands, and therefore have no wood for scaffolding to support the builders above that height—"

"And what of Nectan's dun?" Niall interrupted. "What of the defense wall around it, which is more than twice the height of a man? We managed to collect enough driftwood to construct scaffolding for *that* task of building!"

"True," Coll agreed. "But that wood was collected over a long time and with much labor, and it would require many such duns to shelter the whole tribe. And so there you have my chief problem in designing the Stronghold. How can I build a high, circular tower—a very high tower—and build it quickly, without the aid of any wooden scaffolds to support the builders while they work? And I think I am now very close to solving that problem!"

Niall's impatient look had turned to one of interest by this time, and now he asked curiously, "*How* will you solve it?"

"I will show you that," Coll promised, "very shortly, once the idea I am working on is complete. Then you could show the other members of the Council, and persuade them that every settlement of the tribe must have its own Stronghold against the raiders!"

"He would have to persuade Nectan to listen to him first," Clodha intervened, but Niall shook his head.

"How can anyone explain anything to Nectan in his present mood?" he asked. "If he will not listen even to Anu he will certainly not discuss this with me—or with you either, Coll."

That was the snag, Coll admitted to himself, the snag in all their plans. And there was no way of overcoming it until Nectan himself chose to come out of his shell of silence. Fand's voice, gently mourning, voiced the end of his train of thought.

"Nectan is changed, a changed man, since Domnall set the black dog of despair on him. He will not listen to any of us now."

"And Anu," Clodha pointed out, "will make sure Niall does not approach any other member of the Council without his consent."

Coll glanced a wry agreement to this. Clodha had wisdom, he conceded, although she was only a year older than Fand. It was fortunate she was the one who also had the duty of marrying the proper sort of man to succeed Nectan as Chief!

"Besides," Niall harked back to an earlier point in the discussion, "you have not said you have solved the problem of building high; only that you are on the point of solving it. And there must be many more such problems to overcome before you can claim that your Stronghold is a perfect defense."

"The height is the only one that matters," Coll told him. "I will have the answer to all the others when I have the answer to that one."

"But meanwhile," Clodha said flatly, "you need more time. And so there is still no third choice for the tribe."

Coll stared at her, with arguments rising in his mind and raging there for utterance. Then hopelessly he asked himself how he could even begin to express such arguments. He *knew* that a certain breadth of foundation would carry a certain weight and height of wall on it! He *knew* how far a certain curve could support its own line. He knew an endless number of things about dry-stone building; but they were all discoveries made over years of patient trial and error, and there were simply no words to describe such discoveries. He shrugged, letting his silence be taken for the silence of acceptance. Clodha turned away from him; but with a flush of annoyance beginning to color the pale oval of her face and an unusual sharpness in her voice, Fand said,

"You have not given this enough attention, Clodha. Coll is very clever, and—"

"And Fand is very loyal!"

Sharply Clodha interrupted her sister. There was a small, surprised silence then, as all four of them realized how unexpectedly close they had come to a quarrel. And still nothing useful had come from their meeting, Coll thought in dismay. He bent his head down to his work and was glad of the diversion when Niall exclaimed,

"There is Neith—look! And Drostan, too—coming back from the hunt."

The other three followed his pointed direction and saw the two hunters coming along the ridge behind the bay. A third figure came into view, and Coll remarked,

"I see that Taran is with them again."

"I do not like that man," Clodha said decisively, and Niall turned in surprise to ask,

"But why not?"

Clodha looked sullen, and Niall persisted, "He *is* one of us, after all, is he not? And he behaves as one of us."

"Oh yes," Clodha agreed ironically. "He is brave. He bathes often, as we do, and eats cleanly. Moreover, he is not quarrelsome, as so many of our people are. He does not drink to excess, as so many of them do. And he is not more than ordinarily vain—at least, he is content not to be one of those who are forever seeking good looks by bleaching their hair yellow!"

Niall pounced on her reply. "There you are! On your own saying he shows many of the good points of our people, and few of their bad ones."

"But I forgot to mention," Clodha continued her ironic account, "that Taran is also clever. Clever enough to know that Neith and Drostan are our best hunters, and to take every chance of learning their skills."

"For which he should be praised, Clodha," Niall retorted, "and not condemned."

"Oh, Niall, you are simple!" Clodha clicked her tongue in exasperation. "I would praise Taran—if I thought he had any good motive in setting himself to learn from men like Neith and Drostan. But I do not trust the way he watches and listens and learns from *everything* he has seen since he returned to the islands. He is too intent about it—too eager to learn; and that makes me uneasy, whatever you may think about it."

"I think you are being fanciful," Niall told her sharply.

As if to give point to this reproof, he waved and hallooed to the hunters. They looked in the direction of the shout, but when he waved again and they altered course towards the beach, Fand exclaimed,

"Oh, Niall! This is our private place, and I do not like Taran either. He speaks to me as if I were a child."

"You are a child," Niall teased good-naturedly; but with swift anger, Clodha came to Fand's defense.

"My sister is of marriageable age," she flashed at Niall, "and she is next to me in the line of inheritance. Taran should show more respect to her, and so should you!"

Niall flushed scarlet at her tone, but before either of them could speak again, Coll intervened sharply.

"In the name of the gods, what has happened to friendship when *we* four suddenly quarrel like this? Make your peace with Clodha, Niall. And leave Fand be, or you shall answer to me for it."

Niall and Clodha glanced at one another with expressions of shame on their faces, and speaking quietly to Fand herself, Coll added, "Some men mistake gentleness for foolishness, Fand. Let Taran see you know that, and he will pay the respect due to your true nature."

The hunters were up on them by this time, throwing down the deer carcass they carried. Neith and Drostan came swaggering forward in the manner of men well used to honorable recognition of their skills, and with all their customary cheerfulness. Taran followed more modestly, and with a backward jerk of his thumb Drostan remarked of him,

"He learns quickly!"

Neith nodded agreement, and added, "He will soon be as fast on his feet as we are—and as powerful with a spear!"

Taran looked even more modest at this, but he answered Niall's questions eagerly enough, and the two of them were still deep in conversation by the time Neith and Drostan were prepared to move on again. They picked up the deer, and Drostan called to Taran,

"Remember you promised to skin this beast."

Taran glanced over his shoulder. "And remember you promised I could keep the skin for myself!" he retorted.

Neith and Drostan laughed together at this and, with some further shouted ribaldry, went on their way. Taran turned to finish what he had been saying to Niall, and as Coll resumed his interrupted work of building, it occurred to him how strange Taran's speech sounded compared to their own.

It was the same language, of course, he thought; for that was something the people of the Boar had always had in common with the other Celtic tribes of Britain and Gaul. But Taran spoke it with an accent that was foreign to the islands. Nor did his speech have any of the words of the old tongue in it—the tongue that belonged to the days of the people who had once welcomed the wandering Men of the Boar to the Orkneys, and become one tribe with them.

Taran's long stay in Gaul must have wiped such words from his memory, Coll concluded, then smiled to think that the name "Taran" itself was the word the old tongue had for "thunder."

"But of course," Taran finished what he had been saying, "it was only on the journey home that I began to learn how to hunt; and I would not have deserved any praises then, I can tell you, for slaving as a field hand was no preparation for such skills!"

Niall nodded in sympathy, then curiously he asked, "When did you first make up your mind to escape?"

"The day I was captured." Taran was silent a moment after his reply, then he added, "But every day I spent in Gaul, I looked north across the sea to the mainland of Britain; and every day I swore again to escape across that channel of sea."

"Is it true what the traders say about the legions of Rome?" Coll joined in the conversation. "Do they truly love their war leader—this Chief they call Caesar?"

Taran laughed. "I would not say that Julius Caesar is loved by the legions—admired, certainly, but not loved."

"Have you seen him?" Niall asked.

Taran nodded. "Once. He is a bald, ugly man, very foulmouthed; a clever, cruel, powerful man. I admired him."

"And is it true," Coll pursued, "that his legions number many, many thousands of men?"

"More than you could imagine," Taran told him grimly. "And make no mistake about it, Domnall is right when he says they will invade both the mainland of Britain and its islands some day—if not under this Caesar, certainly under the commander who succeeds him. The prize is too good for them to ignore, now they have reached so close to it."

"Perhaps." Coll shrugged. "And perhaps not. Perhaps some of the stories we hear of Roman power are only travelers' tales that grow with the telling—and even for the big boats of the traders, these islands are more than two moons' sailing from Gaul."

"I had no time to invent travelers' tales," Taran said dryly, "even though my journeying took two years instead of two moons. I was too busy trying to survive in that crazy little boat I stole for the voyage."

Fand said with a shiver, "Two years of sailing by night, and hiding ashore by day! Small wonder you looked so wild when you landed here."

"I looked wilder still, I daresay," Taran told her condescendingly, "when I was grubbing along beaches for food; for I never knew what warlike men I might encounter then. And so, hungry as I often was, I could never risk landing where there was any sign of human life in case a spear in the throat would be my greeting."

He sat back, looking to see the effect of these remarks, and Coll thought how different he looked now from the wild and almost naked stranger of six months ago; for now that his hair was oiled and smoothly flowing from under the bronze fillet holding it in place, the handsome set of his features was clearly evident, and the short tunic he wore set off his powerful figure to its best advantage. Moreover, there was no doubting now that he was a courageous and clever man—the embodiment, in fact, of everything that was admired in the tribe of the Boar. And yet—

Perhaps Clodha was right, Coll decided. Perhaps Taran was too good to be true, too clever on his own account. . . .

Niall was speaking by this time, half admiring also, half laughing as he said, "Well, you know by this time how lucky you were not to get such a greeting from us!"

Taran shrugged. "You could not have killed me," he declared. "Not while I had this talisman gripped in my hand."

Reaching, as he spoke, for a thong of deerskin around his neck, he displayed a little bag the thong had held suspended inside his tunic. With a swift gesture, then, he pulled the bag open and tipped some object from it into his hand. Palm open, he held the object out to view.

It was a stone, a round, translucent stone with a smoothly gleaming surface. Its color was a rich, dark red, and it glowed against the skin of his palm like a small captured piece of an angry winter sunset.

"A carnelian," Niall said with a touch of awe in his voice, and proudly Taran added,

"The stone that has power to guard against all sickness and every kind of evil spirit!"

Clodha looked enviously at him. "You are lucky to have such a talisman," she remarked, and to the murmur of agreement from Coll and Niall, Fand asked,

"But how did you come by it?"

"The gods gave it to me," Taran answered gravely. "I was searching a beach for the ebb-tide food one day long after my escape, and I found it among the pebbles cast up by the tide there. That was when I *knew* I would reach home safely."

Clodha reached out as if delicately to lay a finger on the stone, then hesitated, a mute question in the upward glance of her dark eyes. Taran nodded the permission her eyes asked, and flushing pink with pleasure, Clodha touched the stone. As she drew back her hand, her glance met Taran's again, and softly he said,

"The stone is my good fortune, Clodha, and that is something I would share with you. Take it, and wear my fortune for your ornament."

Clodha's face went rigid with astonishment. Then, with her color rising again, she glanced at Niall. Taran continued to hold out the carnelian, apparently unaware of the offense he had given, and in a voice that was heavy with anger, Niall said,

"You have been long away from the tribe, Taran; long enough perhaps to forget certain things. And because of that, I will pardon you."

Clodha and Fand had scrambled to their feet as he spoke, and as they moved off in the direction of the settlement, he stalked indignantly after them. Coll rose to go also, and Taran remarked,

"So you take one another's quarrels upon you!"

"We are friends." Coll spoke coldly, with a parting

glance of dislike on the words. To his surprise, then, he saw that Taran was smiling as he slipped the carnelian back into its deerskin bag, and with sudden anger he accused.

"You have not forgotten the rule! You *knew* that a Chief's daughter may only accept a gift from the man she is to marry!"

Taran glanced up, cool mockery in his eyes. "I also remember," he remarked, "that a Chief must have the Council's agreement to his choice of husband for a daughter, and Nectan has still to receive that agreement for Niall."

Coll stared at the handsome face looking so calmly up at him; and like one who reads the map of an unknown country, slowly tracing its main routes and features, he read the lines of greed and ambition on it.

"So this is why you came back," he said slowly, "to seek power in the tribe!"

Taran laughed. "I have lived in places and seen sights you could not even begin to imagine," he said. "I have seen power in such places—real power—not the petty kind a man can achieve in these islands!"

"But there was no power of any kind for you in those places, was there?" Coll asked. "You were a slave, Taran. Even after you escaped, you were still not free, for then you were a man wanted for murder. And so you came back here."

"I came home," Taran retorted. "That was a natural thing to do, was it not? To come back to my own people?"

"It was," Coll agreed. "But then you found your Chief's eldest daughter grown to the age of marriage.

And so now you seek to become Chief in his place through marriage to her."

The lazy mockery had faded off Taran's face; but still he kept his voice light, striving for an appearance of indifference as he said, "You seem to place great store on power, Coll. But why should you suppose I think as you do?"

"Because the taste of power is very sweet to a man who has been a slave for half his life," Coll told him. "And you are naturally the kind of man who cares for power."

"You are clever, Coll," Taran said softly. "Your mind is not crippled! I wonder if you will be clever enough not to tell Niall of your opinions."

"I have already told you," Coll said. "Niall is my friend. I shall speak what I please to him."

Taran's hand slid down to the short, broad-bladed knife at his belt. Slowly he withdrew the knife from its sheath; and slowly, still keeping his eyes fixed on Coll, he began to rise.

"Remember that I am the Chief's foster son!" His voice sharp, Coll threw out the warning. "It would be a mistake to kill me, Taran."

Taran was on his feet now. "Who spoke about killing?" he asked. "I was thinking about something quite different, Coll. I was thinking, in fact, about a man I knew once—a man who suffered an accident."

Gently, with the tips of his fingers, he caressed the knife's sharp, heavy blade, and continued, "This man stumbled and fell one day, Coll, on just such rough ground as we stand on now. And as he fell, by a terrible stroke of fortune, his teeth went right through his tongue and he bit the tip of it right off!"

"You are mad!" Coll exclaimed, but Taran only smiled the smile that gave a touch of cruelty to his features.

"Do you know," he asked, "how difficult it is to speak with only half a tongue? That man tried, of course. He tried hard, but his words came out all chewed and mangled and no one could understand—"

Abruptly, as Coll seized a stone from the pile beside him, Taran stopped speaking, and Coll grasped the opportunity to warn him, "Niall and the others are still within earshot, Taran. They could be here in time to see signs of a struggle, and *then* you could not pretend there had been any 'accident.'"

"Shout now, then," Taran invited. "Cry out for help, and let everyone know you are a coward as well as a cripple!" He took a step forward, laughing soundlessly at the flush sweeping over Coll's face. "So you are not a coward," he taunted. "That is good, Coll. I do not like to stain my knife with a coward's blood."

He raised his knife arm and Coll tightened his grip on the stone. He would manage only one strike with it, he calculated, before Taran's superior weight had him pinned; but if he aimed for the head and struck hard enough, he would have a chance of escape. He saw the bulge of muscle on Taran's knife arm become suddenly tense, and heard him say, 1798803

"There is not room in this tribe for two men with clever tongues, Coll."

The blood began to pound in his ears, and through the roaring noise it made, he heard another voice shouting,

"Touch Coll with that knife, and you will die for it!"

His head jerked toward the sound. He was aware of Taran's head turning sharply toward it also, and in the same moment, a stone came hurtling through the air. The aim behind it had force and accuracy and the stone hit Taran heavily on the forehead. He swayed from the impact, tottered a step or two, then sank to his knees and collapsed in a heap at Coll's feet.

In the second or two before Taran was brought to his knees, Coll's eyes roamed frantically over the great tumble of rock that marked the path of the stone's flight; and with a quick shock of recognition as Taran dropped senseless, he saw who had felled him.

There was a boy in a brownish-red cloak poised on the rocks—a boy a few years younger than himself. He was only twenty feet away, and Coll's swift glance at him took in a pale face and straight hair so richly thick and fair that it looked like a helmet of gleaming gold set on his head. Gray eyes, large and peculiarly brilliant in the pale face, flashed an answering signal of recognition at him and the boy called,

"Have I killed him?"

Taran was far from dead, but he was still unconscious. A brief examination was enough to tell Coll this, and he looked up with the information ready on his lips, but the words were never uttered for there was no one to hear them. The boy had vanished as unexpectedly as he had appeared.

Surprise held Coll briefly motionless, then quickly he started forward to scan the waste of rocks ahead; but the color of the boy's cloak was a perfect camouflage against the brownish-red of the sandstone. Disappointedly, Coll searched for some further sign of him and saw a betraying gleam of golden hair. His gaze followed it and made out the figure of the boy leaping nimbly from rock to rock as he retreated farther and farther along the beach.

"Wait!" Coll shouted. "Come back! Come back!" Even as the words left his lips, however, he knew there would be no response to them, and as the last flickering trace of the boy vanished from sight, he turned reluctantly back to Taran again.

The knife that would have mutilated him lay a few feet from the unconscious body, and bending to retrieve it, Coll reflected that Niall would have to be told of Taran's secret designs and ambition. He stuck the knife in his belt and, with all the questions he would have liked to ask his rescuer churning about in his mind, began walking homeward to the settlement.

3
Bran

Coll was being watched. He was aware of this at first as no more than a tingling sensation on the back of his neck, an uneasy crawling of his scalp. He began to snatch frequent looks around on the occasions he worked alone at his Stronghold, and sometimes it seemed to him that he had glimpsed a presence lurking somewhere among the surrounding rocks.

He kept silence about these feelings, however, not even speaking to Niall about them, for something told him that some more definite sign of the presence would eventually emerge. And when that happened, he decided, there would be a situation that was very private to himself. He tried to visualize this situation, but there was a memory obscuring his inner sight, the old black memory of that first raid on the island; and once again he was running along the beach screaming, screaming. . . .

Then somewhere above his head, the world exploded into war. Legs caged him in, bare, heavy-muscled male legs. There was a ring and clash of weapons in his ears, and the snarling noises forced from men in the throes of combat. Breathless in the aftermath of his screaming, he sucked in air that stank of men's bodies, of leather, of half-tanned animal skin. He crouched among the leaping, shifting mass of legs, like a small trapped animal trying to make himself even smaller. Then suddenly the battle above him shifted ground, and he was blundering in solitary terror over sand that carried damp, dark-red patches on the pale gold of its churned surface. A body blocked his path, and the dead, blind stare of his father's face registered on his bewildered mind. He wailed feebly, exhaustedly, a wail of longing for the secure refuge of his mother's arms. And miraculously, had no sooner uttered her name than he saw her, clutching his baby brother, Bran, to her breast as she strained toward him. He ran toward her, seeing also, but not understanding, that she was held fast in the grip of two of the raiders. He sobbed, stretching out to clutch at her dress, and burrowing his head through its folds to reach her. A hand wrenched the stuff of the dress from his grip. His mother was dragged backward to the raiders' boat, screaming his name in anguish, pleading with her captors not to harm him. Another hand plucked strongly at his hair. He was swung upward....

The warm, salt taste of blood in his mouth brought Coll back to reality. He licked his lower lip, slowly absorbing the fact that he had bitten right through a fold of its skin, and with a muttered curse at himself, went back to patiently assembling more of the stones he needed for his building.

A flicker of movement among the brownish-red of the

sandstone rocks caught his eye—the flutter of a brownish-red cloak, and the swift vanishing gleam of a golden head. He straightened himself, peering toward the place where he had seen the movement, and knew that this time he had not imagined the presence among the rocks. It was the boy who had saved him from Taran who was there watching him. And that boy was Bran, his younger brother, who had been saved from the raiders by the courage and desperate resource of their mother, Banba.

Carefully setting a course of the stones he had gathered, he recalled the story of Bran as Anu had told it once a year to them all, ever since the time of the first raid.

Domnall had been present when it happened—Anu's story always began with that reminder. And Broichan, the Druid seer, had been there also; for that evening—the second one following the raid—there had been funeral rites for those killed in battle against the raiders, and funeral portents to observe.

"It was then that Bran was found...."

The storytelling voice that Anu always used to tell the history of the tribe sounded again in Coll's ears.

". . . and everyone who was there marveled at the power of Lir, god of the sea, who had helped Banba to save her child; for Bran came floating into the bay in a tiny coracle fashioned from strips of her sealskin cloak, and it was clear to all present that Banba must have worked secretly at making this little coracle after she was carried aboard the raiders' boat. Then she had strapped the child into it and set it adrift at some point where the wind and tides were favorable for carrying it back to our own island. But it was the god, Lir, who had preserved

the child from storms; and Ogham, who found the little coracle floating in the bay, brought it ashore, praising Lir. . . ."

Ogham's voice had been joined by a chorus of praise as the tiny skin boat was passed wonderingly from hand to hand. But Bran had lain quietly in the midst of all the excitement, his golden hair haloed by the long rays of the setting sun, his eyes gazing up with the strange illusion of wisdom sometimes conveyed by the wide-eyed stare of a baby; and Nectan had told Domnall,

"This is Bran, the son of Banba who was captured in the raid, and of Roth who was killed by the raiders."

"And of Lir," Domnall added, "for Lir has given him his life anew. Lir has also been his father! See in him, then, a wonder and a portent, a child of more than human parentage; a child of destiny!"

Broichan, the seer, spoke then with a strange singing note in his voice, his eyes blank, and bright with the light of prophecy.

"Hear the destiny of Bran," the singing voice cried out. "Bran has been saved by a god, so that he may fulfil the purpose of all the gods. And he must live until that purpose is served. Yet still Bran will not go to his final home with the gods except at a moment of his own choosing, and it shall be the actions of his own tribesmen which will create that moment for him. Then shall the wheel be spun full circle, for then shall Bran's destiny be complete and the gods satisfied. . . ."

"Mark this." Domnall spoke low to Nectan as the singing voice died away. "Mark it well and tell it to the people, so that they may know the moment when it comes. But meanwhile, Bran shall live as a Druid lives and learn as a Druid learns. It is fitting that this should be so."

"He has kin," Nectan said in a troubled voice, watching the Druid lift the child from the tribesman's arms; "the only kin left to him from the raid—a five-year-old brother named Coll."

"A Druid has no kin," Domnall said sternly. "This is a lesson that both the child and his brother must learn...."

Absently, Coll smoothed his hand over the surface of the last stone in his course. Nectan and his family, he reflected, had been all the kin he had ever needed from that day. But what of Bran? How had it felt to grow up without parents, without brothers or sisters, without love or friendship of any kind? On impulse, he spoke, turning his head and pitching his voice to carry some little distance away from himself.

"Show yourself, Bran. I know you are there, and I want to talk to you."

"*—talk to you . . .*" The echo of his voice scuttered among the sandstone boulders. No human sound answered it. The *slap-slap* of the tide against the stones, and the mewing of a herring gull, were all that broke the long following silence. Coll turned to his work again, wondering what had impelled him to cry out. His brother was only a figure in a strange story, a figure the tribe looked at with mild curiosity four times a year, when they gathered to meet the Druids for the great sacrificial festivals. Why, then, should he have suddenly felt it was all wrong that this should be so?

"Will you betray me to Domnall if I speak to you?"

The question sounded from behind him, in a voice so low that he scarcely heard it, and surprise froze him for a moment. His heart resumed its beat, but fast now with the excitement mounting in him. Yet for fear of frightening the quiet voice away again, he resisted the temptation to turn his head toward it, and deliberately kept his own voice quiet.

"May the gods hear me, I will not betray you to anyone."

A footstep crunched on the pebbled beach behind him. A cloak fluttered at the edge of his vision, then Bran stood before him. Coll's glance traveled up from the shoes of deerskin, over the close-fitting woolen breeches and the knee-length woolen tunic, and came finally to rest on the pale face in its frame of bright hair. There was no blue tattoo mark on Bran's forehead—no tribal mark of any kind—and suddenly this seemed the strangest thing of all about him. Coll stared at the smooth, unmarked forehead. His eyes met the brilliance of the gray eyes beneath it and he said,

"You have been watching me. You were watching on the day Taran threatened me with the knife."

Bran did not reply to this, but he nodded, and Coll continued, "And you knew then who I was. But how?"

"You caught only one quick glimpse of me that day," Bran reminded him. "But you knew who I was."

"Of course." Coll stared at him. "*Everybody* knows who you are. They must know—for the sake of the prophecy. The whole tribe looks for you, four times a year, at the place of sacrifice. But how did you pick me out from others of my age?"

Bran's glance slid down to rest briefly on Coll's crippled leg, and quietly he said, "It was not difficult."

"I see." Coll felt himself flushing, although there had been no pity in Bran's glance, and with a touch of annoyance in his voice he asked, "Is that why you threw the stone at Taran? To save a cripple?"

"To save my brother," Bran corrected.

"But—" Coll paused, frowning his bewilderment. "A Druid has no kin," he reminded Bran. "Domnall told Nectan so, the day the Druids claimed you for their own."

"I know that."

Bran spoke with an oddly wistful expression on his face, and Coll remembered that he had wondered what it felt like to grow up without kin, or even friends. So, he told himself, *that* was the answer! It was simple loneliness that had led Bran to spy on himself! He nodded toward a flat boulder beside him, and said dryly,

"Sit down, then. If you are going to defy Domnall's ruling, you may as well do so in comfort."

Bran smiled broadly at this, and the smile made him look so much more like any cheerful fourteen-year-old that Coll felt the last awkwardness between them vanishing. As Bran seated himself, he asked,

"How much more do you know about me?"

"Only what I have guessed from listening to your conversations here," Bran said frankly. "I know that the young warrior Niall is your friend, and that you were brought up in Nectan's household with Clodha and Fand. I know that Niall and Clodha intend to marry, and that Fand is the one—"

"Fand is like a sister to me!" Coll broke in roughly, and then regretted the violence of his tone as Bran flushed burning red and flinched back from him. In a quieter voice, he said,

"You must understand, Bran, that no man can choose

his sons, but he *can* choose whom his daughters will marry. That is why the succession goes through the women of a Chief's line, and that is why Fand must be like a sister to me."

He glanced at Bran's scarlet face and tried to smile reassurance, but in spite of himself, the smile was a twisted one, and his tone was bitter as he added,

"A Chief's daughter must choose her husband from among the best, the bravest, the strongest of men—from among those who can ensure the safety of the tribe. And I am not of that number."

Bran made no immediate answer to this, but after a moment or so he said,

"I understand that, but I cannot feel it. I only know what it is like to live as a Druid lives."

Coll glanced up curiously from the stone he was setting. "And how *does* a Druid live?"

"Painfully!" Bran's grin flashed out at him again, and this time it was a grin of self-mockery. "Learning all the time. Learning mathematics, magic, poetry, prayers. Learning in company with others. Learning alone—learning to be alone, alone in the Ring...."

His voice trailed into silence and Coll continued to stare at him, but in his mind's eye now he was seeing the great ring of upright stones where the Druids held sacrificial festival—sixty of the stones, each of them more than the height of three men, and all of them weathered by the bleak moorland winds sighing constantly around them. The focus of his gaze came back to Bran's face, and with awe touching his voice, he asked,

"Are you not afraid of that—to be alone in the Ring?"

"Why should I be afraid?" Bran's self-mocking smile

flashed out again. "I am a child of destiny, am I not? My time, when it comes, will not find me alone in the Ring, but with all the tribe of the Boar there to see and mark the moment."

"But the Ring is such a lonely place," Coll persisted. "That wind sighing always around the stones, the strange ghostliness of the bird cries that come from the marshes around them—a man would need much courage to be alone there."

"No," Bran said quietly. "It is not courage that is needed, for a man cannot fight the wind or escape from the voices of ghosts. Surrender is the key, brother Coll. I have learned this. I have learned to let my mind drift with the wind and listen to the ghosts. I have learned to be nothing, as the wind is nothing; to step outside my body and be a grass bending in the wind, a bird soaring, a stone rooted deep in the earth. I have learned to be nothing, and everything."

It was impossible to take his eyes off Bran now, Coll found. As if mesmerized, he stared at the pale face, the dreaming look in the huge, brilliant, gray eyes, and then was almost shocked as Bran smiled again suddenly, and with a return to his light mocking voice, said,

"The only thing I have not learned is to be an ordinary person—like any other of my age."

"But there is nothing to learn about that!" Coll exclaimed. "A boy plays, he kicks a ball, he wrestles, plays ball-and-stick, imitates the men with spear and shield, runs with his hound—all as natural as breathing!"

"You are talking about a child growing up among other children—about friendship," Bran said quietly. "And I have known none of that."

There was no self-pity in Bran's voice, Coll realized;

but the wistful look had come back to his face, and impulsively he asked, "Would you run from *my* friends if they were here with me?"

"From Niall?" Bran asked. "And Fand and Clodha?"

Coll nodded. "They would not betray you to Domnall, any more than I would."

"Or be afraid of me?" Bran asked ironically. "I *am* a Druid, after all, brother, and I have learned powers that are—" He hesitated, and then finished, "—unusual."

Coll glanced at him, guessing at the willpower that had hidden the longing behind the ironic tone. "I do not think you are likely to turn such powers against me or my friends," he said steadily. "And if I do not fear you, why should they?"

"Do you mean," Bran asked cautiously, "that you would treat me like one of yourselves?"

"Why not?" Calmly selecting a stone, Coll went on with his building. "That is what you want, is it not?"

There was silence for several moments, then Bran said, "I heard you telling Niall about your Stronghold. Have you managed yet to solve the problem of building high?"

Coll laid another stone, smiling to himself at Bran's roundabout way of answering "yes" to his question. He stepped back to view his handiwork, and wondered if he should tell Bran that he had indeed solved this problem. He had meant Niall to be the first to know, he reminded himself, but it would be another day before Niall was back from the hunt, and this would be an opportunity to tell *someone* of his success! He looked up to see Bran intently watching him, and said briskly,

"Yes, I have the answer now. Watch, and I will explain it." Rapidly he fitted the last course to the circular wall he had been building, and told Bran, "There is the base of my tower now—a solid wall of stone built in the shape of a circle enclosing a central courtyard. You see?"

Bran nodded, and asked, "But how high will this base be in the real tower? And how thick?"

"Twice the height of a man," Coll told him, "and it will be as thick as it is high. Now, notice how flat and level I have made the top surface of this base, and watch the next step in the construction!"

With careful fingers, then, Coll began edging both the inner and the outer perimeters of the tower's base with a parapet of stones, and neatly bridged the space between these two parapets with a roofing of stones specially selected for their flat surface.

"You see?" he asked again. "I have built a roofed gallery on to the base of this little tower. And when it comes to making the real tower, the builders will have the flat platform of its base to stand on in order to construct the real version of this gallery. Now watch me raise a second gallery on top of the roof of the first one."

Swiftly he built another double parapet around the inner and outer perimeters of the gallery's roof, and bridged the space between the two parapets with more of the flat stones. Then once again he turned to Bran.

"And so," he announced, "the second roofed gallery of my tower is complete! And when it comes to building the real tower, the men working on it will stand on the roof of its first gallery to build the real version of this second gallery."

"And so on to a third gallery?" Bran asked.

Coll paused in selecting more of the flat stones. "I have worked out that I can go up to eight galleries," he said proudly. "That will make the total height of the Stronghold more than the height of ten men. And not one single wooden support will be needed to let the builders reach this height, for each gallery will be built by men standing on the roof of the one below it."

"But you told Niall you would have to be able to build your Stronghold quickly," Bran exclaimed. "And think of the time it would take to lay the stone for all these galleries!"

"I have thought of that," Coll told him, "and I have given an inward curve to the Stronghold's outer wall, from about the height of the third gallery. Thus, the higher the tower goes, the less stone will be needed to make the outer walls of these galleries—which will not only speed up the work of construction, but will also reduce the total weight the base will have to carry."

"But how will it be possible to pass from one gallery to another?" Bran asked. "Have you thought of that?"

"I have thought of everything!" Coll looked up, with a grin that took the boast out of his words. "There will be a stairway projecting from the inner face of the outside wall, and winding around this inner face so that it passes through each of the galleries in turn—right to the level of the top gallery."

"Which will not be roofed, I suppose?" Bran ventured; and Coll agreed,

"Of course not; for that is where the main force of the defenders will make their stand!"

He bent to his building again. Bran watched him in silence, noting how sure his eye was for the line of the stones, how ingeniously he fitted one upon another. But that was the least of Coll's gifts, Bran told himself. It was

49

a brilliant concept—this system of galleries within a hollow-walled structure!

And yet, it was such a simple one—or, at least, it seemed simple now that Coll had explained so clearly how each stage of building his Stronghold would be the platform for the next stage. Why had no one ever thought of that before? Why had no one else in these treeless islands realized that the structure of a stone building could provide its own scaffolding?

A recollection of Domnall's teaching flashed into Bran's mind, and answered all his questions. Because that was the way with all great ideas, he reminded himself. They seemed simple only because they rested on principles that could be demonstrated to be true. But it took a really great mind in the first place to recognize the mere existence of such principles!

Curiously, Bran studied Coll's face; and wonderingly he noted the tenseness in the angular planes of its thin, weather-beaten features, the determination in the firm line of the mouth. His gaze came finally to rest on Coll's eyes, still intently fixed on his tower, and his wonder grew at the power of thought that had conjured an idea as original as the Stronghold out of this little heap of stones. Quietly he said,

"I am honored you have shown me your idea, Coll. It is a brilliant one."

Coll glanced up, with wry good humor in his face. "Let us hope that Nectan agrees with you," he remarked. "And also that both he and Domnall will see how the Stronghold can provide a middle road between their opposing policies!"

Rising to his feet, then, he dusted away the powdery film the sandstone had left on his hands, and turned to look thoughtfully seaward. There was a flight of eider ducks close inshore, diving for food and surfacing bouncily again. The wind that blew so often over the islands was a gentle one that day. He watched the ducks without seeing them, and was conscious of the wind's soft passage without feeling it. There was a peace on him, the island peace that comes from the spaciousness of sea and sky all around; and an inner peace also, that came from the sense of a long task accomplished at last. He savored the feeling, luxuriated in it, and was roughly jolted out of it again by Bran's voice.

"There will be no taking of any middle road if Taran has his way."

"Taran?" Coll whipped round, staring at Bran. "What has Taran got to do with this?"

"I should not have spoken."

Bran rose to his feet with the words, and stood looking distractedly around. He was contemplating flight, Coll realized, and in another moment he would be gone—perhaps never to be seen again! He lunged forward to grasp him, but Bran was the quicker of the two. He leaped clear of Coll's reaching hands and said rapidly,

"It is Druid business. I cannot say anything else."

With an effort Coll suppressed the angry retort that rose to his mind. Through stiff lips, he said,

"I have worked for thirteen years to design this Stronghold, and now that I have succeeded, it could save many lives."

Bran made no answer to this, and Coll tried again. "You came here seeking friendship," he said accusingly, "and I gave that to you. I told you things I have not even spoken about to Niall as yet."

Still Bran made no answer, but he was making no

further move to escape, and there was a hunted look on his face now. Coll tried one last appeal.

"We are brothers, Bran, and that tie is the strongest one on earth. You proved that today, did you not, when you came to see me? You had to defy Domnall's ruling to do that."

"I—" Bran hesitated, licking his lips uncertainly, and then blurted out, "I know. I know that! But you forget, I am not like you. I am a Druid. And more than that, I am marked for destiny. I *must* follow the path Domnall has set for me. I *must* throw in my lot with him."

"No, Bran, no!"

Coll spoke quietly, rapidly, inching nearer to Bran with the words. "You are my brother. Follow my path. Throw in your lot with me, and Niall, and Clodha and Fand. Be one of us!"

"Is that the price—to tell you about Taran?" Bran's pale face went even paler. A huge misery looked suddenly out of his brilliant gray eyes, but steeling himself against that look, Coll said,

"It is always the price of friendship—to share, to be loyal, to give and receive perfect trust. We cannot accept you without that price."

"You said there was nothing to learn about being ordinary." Bran's lips twisted in a bitter little smile as he spoke. "But you were wrong, brother. You were wrong. And this is a painful lesson."

"Tell me." Coll held Bran's gaze with his own, and with a shrug Bran yielded at last.

"Taran is plotting with Domnall against Nectan," he said. "All this winter he has been coming to visit Domnall, and from their looks now I think that whatever plan they have had in mind has been laid."

With an abrupt gesture he turned to walk away, but Coll was near enough now to lay hold of him, and, shooting out a hand to grasp Bran's shoulder, he demanded,

"Is that all you know?"

"That is all."

"And will you help Niall and myself to find out more?"

A quiver ran through the thin shoulder under Coll's hand, then Bran turned his head and looked full at him.

"You named the terms and I accepted them," he said harshly, "but they are the same for you as for me. Do me the goodness to believe I will keep my part of the bargain."

Then he was gone, wrenching his shoulder free and making off across the rocks with the agility of a hunted deer.

"Bran—wait!" Coll shouted after him, but the flying feet did not pause; and not even when he shouted appealingly, "Brother—!" did Bran throw a single backward glance at him.

4
Expedition

Along the length of the low table that held the remains of the supper feast, Niall's glance met that of Coll. *"Be ready!"* Niall's eyes warned, and with the briefest of nods, Coll acknowledged the message.

It was the tail end of an evening in Nectan's dun. The womenfolk had long since withdrawn from the company, and the leather curtains over the married women's quarters were closed. All the storytelling was at an end, the music of harp and pipes silenced. The young men who had displayed their skill in wrestling were sprawled again beside their elders, and indolently finishing the last of their barley beer.

Niall rose, yawning, and strolled toward the open door of the dun. Coll stayed where he was, apparently half asleep as he stared into the glow of the peat fire in the central hearth beyond the table. Niall stopped to speak to the guard on duty at the door. Coll tossed a bone from the table to one of the dogs prowling restlessly near him, and under cover of the gesture, flicked a glance at the situation inside the dun.

Faces leaped briefly out at him, flushed with satisfied appetite and highlighted by the smoky glow of the whale-oil lamps set into the surrounding walls. He caught the gleam of an enameled shoulder brooch, a glint of silver thread on the neck of a tunic, the flash of a bronze drinking cup raised. He saw Taran staring absently into space and, rising casually as Niall had done, wondered how long it would be before they discovered the plans hiding behind that brooding stare.

Moving silently on the rushes underfoot, he began sauntering toward the door, then became aware of Nectan's eyes on him. He moved closer in response to their beckoning look. Nectan's gaze dropped again to the bronze pieces on the chessboard in front of him. He spoke low, so low that Coll had to lean over his shoulder to catch what was said.

"I am not blind, Coll. I know that you and Niall have been up to something these past few nights, and I do not give my permission for it. You understand?"

"We will tell you when the time comes, and our intent is good."

Coll answered in the same low tones, making a pretense of studying the pieces on the board as he spoke, and Nectan continued,

"Very well. But I suspect that this secret ploy has something to do with the situation between Domnall and myself. And so know this, both of you. I have finally decided that I will defy Domnall's curse, and nothing now can alter that decision."

Coll straightened up, his heart suddenly racing; but he

kept his eyes on the board and as Nectan moved his Queen piece he answered cryptically,

"Yes—yes, I see the reason for your move."

"Check, and—*checkmate!*"

The sound of Nectan's opponent announcing his countermove came triumphantly to him—like a voice of ill omen exulting over what might happen now, he thought uneasily, and brooded on this as he continued toward the door.

Niall was still there, talking to the guard on duty, and he nodded a brief good-night to them both. Niall said, "I'll join you, Coll," and together they stepped off into the darkness beyond the door.

Forty feet ahead of them now loomed the curve of the dun's outer defense wall, with its gate barred and guarded for the night. A guard, holding a leash of watchdogs in check, challenged them briefly from the direction of the gate. They stopped to call an answer and heard, through the silence that followed, a rippling strain of harp music and the sound of a voice singing. The sound came from the young unmarried women's quarters built against the inner side of the defense wall's eastern aspect, and Coll smiled to himself in the darkness as he recognized the high, sweet voice of Fand.

He moved with Niall toward the west side of the enclosure, where the young bachelor quarters were similarly built against the inner side of the defense wall. There was a light glowing here, and passing under the stone piers that raised the row of cubicle-like apartments high above ground level, they heard laughter and the sound of a dice game in progress.

Niall took the lead up the ladder swinging from the

entrance to the sleeping quarters he shared with Coll and, with the deftness of practice, began removing a section of the thatch that roofed the small stone cubicle. Coll followed him up, then unhooked the ladder and rolled the length of its pliant leather structure into a tight bundle. Niall finished removing the section of thatch, and gray light filtered in on them.

"Niall . . ." Coll peered toward the shadowy figure the light showed him. "I have something to tell you."

Niall turned toward him, and he continued, "Nectan has been observing us, and he has guessed something of what we are doing. He spoke to me just before I left the dun, and told me that—whatever it is—it will not alter the decision he has finally made. He means to defy Domnall!"

Niall gave a sharp intake of breath. A moment of silence followed, and then he asked, "Do you think that should alter our plans for tonight?"

"No," Coll told him. "I think it makes them more urgent!"

He moved forward. Niall flexed his knees and formed a step with interlocked hands held in front of himself. Coll thrust the coiled ladder inside his tunic and placed one foot on the interlocked hands. Niall straightened, heaving upward, and Coll's head poked through the hole in the thatch.

The outer defense wall was now inches in front of Coll's nose. The top of it was less than a couple of feet above his head. Coll grabbed for the top of the wall and achieved a hold that enabled him to haul himself onto it. Lying flat there, he hooked the ladder on to the wall and let it down to Niall. Seconds later, Niall was also lying flat on the wall and they were reversing the ladder's hold so that it hung down the outside aspect of the wall.

Coll was the first to scramble down to the ditch below the wall. As his feet touched earth he heard the small, scraping sounds of Niall's following progress, and continued cautiously on into the depths of the ditch. Niall caught up with him as he crawled up its farther side. Flat to the earth, they rolled themselves over the lip of the ditch, and began squirming forward to the cover of the rank grass clothing the slope of the ridge beyond it.

It was a movement that Coll found excruciatingly painful; but grimly, as he had done on the past three nights, he set himself to endure the pain. A month of nights like this would be worth it to catch Taran out, he told himself, then heard Niall speaking low in his throat as they reached their temporary shelter.

"This will be the fourth night of waiting, Coll. Are you still sure it will be worthwhile?"

Coll waited a moment to recover his breath, then whispered his reply. "Bran said he has been visiting Domnall all winter, and sooner or later we are bound to catch him at that."

"And then?"

"That is when we will find out if all this has been worthwhile. It will depend on what we discover then!"

They kept still and silent after that, lying prone on the grass with eyes on the wall and ears alert for any prowling step near them.

"There he is!" Niall whispered the warning at last, and for a brief moment they both caught the movement of a dark shape on the wall top—Taran, using the same method of leaving the dun undetected as they themselves had used! Or at least, Coll decided, for lack of any proof to the contrary, they had to assume it was Taran.

With hearing now tuned to its keenest pitch, he followed the tiny sounds of a progress away from the wall of the dun. The sounds came from their left, which meant that the person making them was heading in a north-by-east direction. And that, Coll realized, was the direction taken by the familiar route to the Ring! Motionless, he listened, and waited for Niall to make the next move.

The signal for it seemed a long time in coming, and the last whisper of sound from their left had long since died before he felt the light, quick pressure of Niall's fingers on his arm. Stealthily then, he followed Niall's example, and began rising from his prone position.

What they had to do now was already planned; for if they were right in assuming it was Taran they had seen, they had also to assume that his eventual destination was a meeting with Domnall at the Ring. But if they trailed him to such a meeting, they would risk his discovering that he was being followed; and so there was nothing for it but to arrive at the Ring ahead of him. Unhesitatingly, the two of them began moving north in a line which would cut across the north-by-east arc that the direction of Taran's movement had indicated.

Crouching low, and treading with careful silence, they climbed the ridge behind the settlement. Then, crawling on all fours to avoid being silhouetted against the skyline, they crossed the summit of the ridge. Now there was no danger of being seen from the settlement, and they straightened themselves for a brisk pace across the four miles that lay between them and the Ring.

They were on a beaten track by this time, the track that led through the cultivated land worked by the bondsmen of the tribe; and for the few hundred yards that this lasted, Coll had no trouble in keeping pace with Niall. It was a different matter, however, on the moorland beyond the fields, and as soon as they encountered this rough going he dropped half a pace behind Niall. Then, placing his left hand on Niall's right shoulder so that it acted as a crutch for him, he leaned on his grip and matched his limping step to the other's easy stride.

It was an old and well-tried arrangement, this, and as he swung back into the familiar motions of it, Coll found his mind flashing back to the kind of childish escapade that had tested its value. For a moment he smiled inwardly at passing memories of all the times they had relied on the combination of Niall's strength and his own quick wits to carry them out of trouble; then Niall's voice, sounding low and warningly, brought him back to the present moment.

"There is too much light." Niall glanced skyward as he spoke. "And the wind is too uncertain."

Coll followed his glance toward the three-quarter moon scudding high in the sky. He noted the smoke-thin cover of the clouds drawn raggedly across it, and dismay struck him at the meaning of Niall's remark. With the wind gusting like this, he realized, they could not count on the moon's light being hidden for more than a few seconds at a time. And the great danger of this shorter route to the Ring was that it lay between the hostile territory of the Raven tribe on the one hand, and the equally hostile tribe of the Deer on the other! He glanced sharply around, and sensed something wrong with their direction of travel.

"We will have to pass too close to the Raven settlements on this tack," he warned Niall. "Bear farther east."

Niall grunted agreement, and swung farther to their right. They jogged steadily on, heads turning constantly in survey of the moor humped and hillocked darkly all around. The first mile of moorland dropped behind them. The clouds shifted. The moon peered unfriendly down. They were in Raven territory now, Coll realized, and in the sudden tenseness of the shoulder under his hand, he felt the fear that moved in his own mind.

But there was no reason for either of them to be ashamed of that, he defended the feeling; for who would not be afraid of such uncanny people as the Raven and the Deer? They were the old tribes of the islands, after all; the tribes that had been there long before the Boar came. And they had great knowledge of old ways, a secret knowledge of runes and charms and spells, and every other form of magic.

Coll's skin crept at the thought, and unwelcome pictures began invading his mind. He saw the small, dark people of the Raven and the Deer crouched half underground in the primitive houses they hollowed from the earth and roofed over with a dome of green turf; saw them strangely dressed in colors that blended with the colors of the earth, the women with their hair long and wild, the men wearing pointed caps and armed with the bronze swords of a bygone day.

He saw the herds of small black cattle whose hides they traded in return for the iron swords they coveted so fiercely and could not make for themselves. And remembering how his own people so jealously guarded the secrets of the ironsmith, how often they had stood between the traders and the little people's attempts to barter for the finished weapons, he shivered at the thought of the hidden eyes that might even now be watching him.

The second mile and the third pounded rhythmically past without incident. Then a hare started up almost under their feet, and as they recovered from the stumble it caused, the betraying moon glided once more into hiding. Coll lost his footing altogether, and gasped at the stab of pain that shot through his damaged hip. Niall turned a questioning face to him.

"Do you want to rest?"

"Go on. We are not out of danger yet."

Coll spoke brusquely to hide his annoyance at himself, but Niall made no retort; and gradually, as the risk of an encounter with a roving band of the Raven or the Deer became less likely, Coll felt a slackening of the tension that had held them both so nerve-stretched. He began to pay more attention to the landscape directly ahead, and as they crossed a ridge of moorland half a mile farther on, a gleam of moonlight-silvered water caught his eye.

The gleam lay to the left of his forward vision, which meant that it came from the nearer of the two shallow lochs forking out like the arms of a Y shape on either side of the moor where the stones of the Ring were planted. Ahead and to the right, then, should be the track leading into the narrow spit of land which separated these two lochs and which formed the stem of this Y shape. And on their near left, on the line of this track, should be the group of four tall stones called the Guard Stones; while on the spit of land itself should be the even taller shape of the single stone called the Gatekeeper.

Niall slowed his step, and Coll adjusted his pace accordingly. The upper parts of the Guard Stones and the

Gatekeeper rose into silhouette against the night sky. Their approach became slower and slower still; a step and a pause to listen, another step and another pause. Coll thought seriously for the first time of the penalties attached to trespassing on a Druid enclosure, and was appalled at the risk they were taking.

Something moved in the gloom ahead—a shadow detaching itself from the infinitely taller shadow of the Gatekeeper. Coll and Niall froze in their tracks. There was no point in flight at that moment. There was no cover to run to! They crouched low, hoping by their stillness to be taken for dark, crouching rocks; but the stranger figure came steadily on toward them as if it knew exactly what they were and who they were. Then some yards away from them, it stopped, and a whispered question came from it.

"Coll . . . ? Is it you, Coll?"

"Bran!" With a mutter of amazement, Coll nudged Niall and repeated, "Bran! That was Bran's voice!" The figure began moving forward again, and he sent an answering whisper to it,

"Yes, it is Coll. And Niall also."

"I have been waiting for you," Bran's further whisper reached him; then the two of them were face to face, peering through the darkness at one another as Bran crouched on a level with him.

"I guessed you might come," Bran continued, "because I knew that Taran was coming to the Ring tonight. I guessed you might follow him, and so I waited here for you."

"Is he here already?" Coll asked in surprise. "We came by a shorter way, hoping to arrive before him."

"Which you have done," Bran told him. "But Taran will not be the only stranger at the Ring tonight. Deva, the Chief of the Raven, and Arcon, Chief of the Deer, will also be coming to talk with Domnall."

"And their visit has some connection with Taran. Is that what you mean?"

Bran hesitated. "I think it must have," he said slowly. "Domnall said something that made me think Taran is proposing an alliance of the Boar with the Raven and the Deer."

"What sort of alliance?" Niall pressed closer to join the whispered conversation, and Bran told him,

"One that will enable the Boar to fight the raiders as Domnall wishes them to fight."

"But Taran has no authority to propose any sort of alliance!" Niall exclaimed. "And as for this one—! It is only because Raven has always fought with Deer in the past that we have been able to master them. But Raven joined with Deer can easily defeat the Boar, and then *we* shall be the subject tribe!"

"You must argue all these matters out for yourselves," Bran told him. "But as for Taran's authority, he will have Domnall's backing in anything he does. And there is one thing more I must tell you. Domnall intends that this alliance will give Taran the mastery of your tribe."

Niall's head jerked forward sharply. "How do you know that?"

"I do not *know* it." Bran drew back from the sharp gesture, spreading out his hands helplessly as he answered. "It is just something I have guessed from hearing the way that Domnall spoke of Taran's visit tonight."

"But why?" Niall wondered. "Why should Domnall want Taran as Chief of the Boar?"

"Because Taran is his creature, of course," Coll exclaimed. "And because Nectan is the only Chief in the islands with the courage to defy him."

Bran said quietly, "That is how you choose to see it, but there are other ways. A Chief *must* obey his Druid in matters of faith, and if Nectan will not give that obedience, Domnall is bound to seek to replace him with another who will."

There was a moment's uneasy silence, with neither Coll nor Niall knowing how to reply to this. Then Niall told Bran,

"Nevertheless, we must still try to find out more about this matter. Can you help us? Can you show us where we can overhear them talking?"

"No!" Bran backed in alarm from him. "You cannot set foot in the Ring! It would be desecration. And you would be discovered for certain. The signs are that the clouds will clear shortly, and then the sky will be bright enough to show every movement there."

As if to point his words, the moon began slowly sailing out from behind its thin cloud cover and showed their faces to one another. Bran looked frightened, Coll thought compassionately, and very young. But Niall was hawk-faced, on the verge of speaking sharply again, and to forestall his words, Coll said,

"If we come here again, Bran—"

"You must not come here again," Bran interrupted. "You especially, Coll; for if you are discovered here, then Domnall might suspect that I have something to do with it."

"But you are our only link with what is going on," Coll pressed gently. "You see that, do you not? And something may happen that will make it important for us to speak to you."

"There is another way." Bran spoke slowly, as if reluctant to admit what was in his mind. "Do you remember I told you I had learned certain powers from the Druids?"

Coll nodded, and with a hesitant glance at Niall, Bran continued, " 'Unusual' powers, I called them; and this is one of them. If someone empties his mind of all other thoughts and thinks only of one thing, I can feel a picture of that single thought shaping itself in my own mind. Do you understand?"

Coll looked at him in bewilderment. "I—I am not sure," he said. "Are you trying to say that if I thought of something happening far away from you, you would know of it also?"

"No, no, that would be too difficult." Bran gave a tolerant little half smile, as if amused that anyone should find this a problem. "I mean simply that you should think of me, and I would feel your thought in my mind as if you were calling me."

"And you would come?" Coll asked.

"As quickly as I could," Bran answered. "And then you could tell me in words why I was needed."

It was chilly there on the moor, Coll realized suddenly. He became aware of the wildfowl stirring in the marshy verges of the lochs on either side of the Ring, and thought how strange their voices sounded—like ghosts whispering and chuckling together in the darkness. The ghosts of the Ring, he thought, staring at Bran's pale, moonlit face, and wondering why he had ever presumed to pity a creature so mysteriously different from himself. The wind touched him coldly, and he shivered; but Niall was speaking now, and Niall did not seem to be affected by the oddly fey atmosphere that Bran carried with him.

"We are obliged to you, Bran," he was saying. "And you will also be welcome for yourself alone if you wish to come and—"

A whir and a rush of wings from the marshes interrupted him, as a flight of pintail ducks rose suddenly from among the reeds. Bran grabbed Coll's arm and said urgently,

"Down! Down flat! There must be someone coming!"

They were down, all three of them, before Bran had finished speaking, lying flat on their faces among a tangle of grass and tough, springy stems of dead heather. They lay still, straining to hear the sound that had alarmed the ducks. Coll fancied he heard voices, then, a moment or two later, knew he had been right. He risked raising his head slightly to peer along the line of the track leading toward the Ring. Nothing moved there. He held the position, the muscles of his neck aching with effort, and was suddenly rewarded by the sight of three figures looming up against the skyline.

The middle figure was taller than the one on either side of it. *Taran!* Coll's mind registered, as he ducked again, instantly. With face pressed flat to the ground he recalled the group to his mind's eye, and thought of the small, dark man who was Deva, Chief of the Raven, and that other small, dark man who was Arcon, Chief of the Deer. They must have been the figures flanking Taran, he decided, and wondered at what point of the way they had met.

Had it been an arranged meeting? Or had Deva and Arcon simply appeared like shadows at Taran's side in that soundless, sudden way which was the special talent of the people of the Raven and the Deer? A flicker of the superstitious fear that had gripped him earlier crossed Col's mind, then he felt Bran's lips warm against his ear and heard Bran whispering,

"Deva and Arcon are keen-scented as hounds. No use to hide when they can smell our presence. But I can divert them and that will let you escape."

Bran was on his feet before there was time to frame an answer to this, and making off with loud, swishing steps through the long grass. Still lying flat and motionless, they heard his voice ring boldly out.

"Who passes the Gatekeeper?"

There was a muddled burst of answer to this challenge, sounds of movement, more voices. The voices rose and fell, grew quieter, receded farther and farther from their hearing. Then finally, there was silence. Coll was the first to move after that. Turning his head sideways in the grass, he whispered to Niall,

"He may have saved our lives there!"

"But the night is not out yet," Niall whispered in reply. "We will take the longer road home—the safer one!"

Cautiously he came to his feet, and Coll rose with him. Keeping low to the ground, they headed side by side for the track leading back to the dun, and straightened up only when they were well beyond any risk of being seen against the skyline.

Neither of them spoke on the homeward journey, although Coll would dearly have loved to voice the thought churning in his mind. But sound at night, he realized, carried too easily to risk any conversation. Niall was equally cautious, and it was only as they approached the dun that he said quietly,

"You deal with the dogs, Coll, while I wake Nectan."

Coll muttered agreement, and in silence after that they recrossed the ditch and scrambled up the ladder they had left hanging down from the wall. Coll took the ladder from Niall and rehung it from the entrance to their sleeping quarters, but even the small, rustling sounds this created were enough to bring the dogs down on them.

The creatures were loose now, freely roaming around the space between the wall and the dun itself, and Niall waited beside Coll to receive their howling rush.

"*Cano! Brecc! Cumhal!*" Sharply Coll spoke their names, and with their howls changing to yelps of recognition, the hounds clustered around them.

"Hush their noise," Niall instructed, and pushed his way past the leaping dogs toward the dun. Coll waited, soothing the yelping forms into silence again; then, gently disengaging himself, he followed Niall. The dogs trailed at his heels, but with a sharp word of command he dismissed them and stepped inside the dun.

Niall was talking in low rapid tones as he entered. Nectan stood beside him, kicking the hearth fire into a blaze, and its light showed Anu as well, crouched down by the fire and huddling a long fur cloak around herself. Their faces turned toward him. He went forward to the fire, not realizing how badly he was limping by this time, and Anu exclaimed sharply.

"You should not have trailed all those miles," she told him. "You were foolish, Coll."

"They were both foolish to go anywhere near the

Ring," Nectan growled, "but thank the gods some good has come of their folly."

"But what will you do about it?" Niall demanded. "This Taran must be checked somehow."

Nectan looked down at Anu. "There is only one way Taran can become Chief," he reminded her, and Anu nodded.

"Clodha," she said. "He means to marry Clodha."

"The girl must be warned then," Nectan continued. "See to it, Anu. And warn Fand also. If anything happens to Clodha, she will be his next aim."

"And the plan for an alliance with the Raven and the Deer," Niall pressed. "What of that?"

"It has its merits as well as its disadvantages," Nectan acknowledged, "and I cannot stop him laying it before the Council. But I can force his hand over that, and have my own counterstroke ready."

"And supposing you succeed with this counterstroke," Niall demanded, "where will that leave us?"

"Where we started," Nectan retorted. "But with this difference—that I intend to have the whole tribe behind me now in my defiance of Domnall! A curse such as he threatened is not worked in a day, Niall, and he cannot blast every single man who supports me. That would stretch even a Druid's magic! And so I will call a muster of the tribe, and that will be my message to them. Stand together on this, and we can risk Domnall's anger."

"But you do not *need* to do that!"

In his growing anxiety to be heard, Coll almost shouted the thought that had occupied him all the way back from the Ring. The other three turned to stare at him, and Nectan frowned his displeasure. But there was no stopping Coll now that his tongue was unloosed.

"I can offer you a middle course, Nectan," he rushed on, "a Stronghold that you can defend against the raiders; a Stronghold from which you can fight, as Domnall wishes you to fight. I have solved all the problems of its building. I have discovered a way. . . ."

Breathlessly he continued, hands building an imaginary tower, voice soaring enthusiastically as he reeled out detail upon detail of his Stronghold's construction. And was almost persuaded that Nectan's continued silence was a sign of his conversion to the idea, until Nectan himself spoke.

"So you want me to back down from the Druid's threat, do you?" Nectan's voice was a rumbling sound that presaged the thunder to come. "All you have learned tonight, all you have come rushing back here to tell me, has taught you nothing. Is that it? You still see this question as a dispute of policy between Domnall and myself?"

Nectan paused to glare at him, and the rumbling voice broke into the threatened thunder. "This is no dispute of policy now! This is a dispute over *power*! Whose power shall rule these islands? Domnall's, through his magic, or through his puppet, Taran? Or mine? Am I to submit to the Druid through fear, or to become just another of his puppets? Or am I to be in very truth the Chief of the Boar? Answer me that, Coll. *Answer me!*"

Coll turned away, despair silencing any reply he might have made. Nectan had not even been listening to his explanation, he realized, and Taran's scheming had destroyed the hope of any other solution to the struggle between Nectan and Domnall. There *was* no answer to Nectan's questions; no way at all for the stubborn will of either Chief or Chief Druid to back away from the final, decisive confrontation.

5
Contest

"A Chief," said Nectan, "must be prepared to act in the grand manner. And when he moves to unmask an enemy, he must do so with speed and decision."

He was standing, as he spoke, in the games enclosure extending on the south side of his dun. The warriors of the Boar, summoned hastily from every settlement of the tribe, were ranked all around him; and perched on the enclosure's wall, well clear of the dangerous event he had planned for that day, were the women and children of his own settlement. Coll and Niall stood with him in the clear space at the center of the enclosure, and listening to the arrogant sound of his words, Coll wondered at the pride that prompted them.

To risk his life and his whole authority over the tribe in one single test of courage—that was indeed acting in the grand manner! But was there not also a very madness of pride in such a gesture? And even if Nectan survived the test he had set himself, supposing that this was still not enough to rally the tribe to his defiance of Domnall? Taran's hand would not be forced then! Indeed, Coll told himself, Nectan's failure in this would be the very opportunity for Taran to succeed in persuading the Council to *his* scheme!

Nectan's hand descended on his shoulder. Nectan's voice jerked him out of his reverie. "And this day," the voice declared, "I shall show Taran what it really means to be a Chief!"

"A lesson that Domnall also will learn," Niall added grimly.

"If he comes at all today," Coll pointed out. "There has been no sign of him as yet."

"Domnall will come," Nectan predicted confidently. "You can depend on it, Coll, that Taran has warned him of this sudden muster; and Domnall will be quick to guess at the reason for it, as Taran must be guessing now."

"But—" Coll hesitated, then plunged boldly on with the doubts crowding his mind. "You are taking a fearful risk, Nectan, and the stakes are high—your life, and your whole authority as Chief. Supposing you lose this gamble!"

"If I am truly a Chief," Nectan told him, "I cannot lose." He drew himself proudly erect with the words, and Coll looked with sudden, fresh realization at the figure towering over him.

Nectan was stripped almost naked for the action he would shortly face. His skin was oiled, and the spring sunlight striking into the enclosure gave his rippling muscles a gleam like that of polished bronze. One hand

73

hung loose at his side. The other gripped a knife with a keen, narrow blade. Yet for all that this was the only weapon he had to fight the most dangerous creature in the islands, his eyes were fearless; the jut of his freshly razored chin was a formidable one.

This, thought Coll in sudden exaltation, was how a Chief should look! This was what he should be—a man supremely confident, a man who outranked all other men in strength and courage. And this was no longer the Nectan who had brooded so sullenly all winter. This was Nectan restored to his former self, and he was truly a Chief!

Niall spoke, breaking the spell of the moment. "Strength to your arm, then, Nectan."

"The gods will give it," Nectan responded.

Niall moved away to take his place with the rest of the Council, and Nectan once more gave his attention to Coll.

"The little one—Fand," he said quietly. "She will be afraid for me today, and a Chief's daughter must not show fear. Will you help her, Coll?"

"I will do everything I can," Coll promised.

Nectan's eyes held his own with a look that seemed to bore down to his most secret thoughts, but Coll kept his gaze steady, and Nectan continued,

"And knowing that a Chief is bound by custom in the question of a daughter's marriage, will you forgive me this and all the other demands I have already made on your kindness to her?"

A man who might be about to die should have no other problems on his mind, Coll told himself. And for Nectan to ask such a question was to admit that he was indeed facing death. He forced his lips to smile, his voice to answer lightly, almost carelessly,

"There is nothing to forgive, Nectan. I have long since accepted that Fand cannot marry a lame man."

"You are a liar, Coll, but a brave one. And I salute you for it."

It never had been possible to deceive Nectan, Coll thought wryly. He acknowledged the thought with a smile that had genuine amusement in it this time, and as Nectan smiled slowly in reply he made his own farewell.

"Strength to your arm, Nectan!"

"The gods will give it."

With Nectan's response still sounding in his ears, Coll limped across the center of the enclosure, and passed through the warriors massed at the foot of the stone dais on its far side. The Council members were all well to the fore at this point, he noted. And, standing among a group of women on the enclosure wall behind them, the herb woman was waiting with her basketful of ointments and clean moss all ready to dress any wounds that Nectan might suffer.

Fand looked anxiously at him as he mounted the first step of the dais to stand beside her, and from the upper level of the dais Clodha leaned down to whisper,

"Is it well with Nectan? Is his courage high?"

"I quote you his own words," he told them both. " 'This day I shall show Taran what it really means to be a Chief!' "

Fand searched his face for further reassurance. "But the danger," she fretted. "And Nectan is no longer a young man!"

"Hush!" Coll gripped her arm gently and nodded toward the six men waiting by the gate of the enclosure. "The trumpeters are ready."

Fand turned to watch the trumpeters raising their instruments high. From the mouth of the weirdly shaped animal head that terminated each trumpet's cone came a harsh, braying note. A deep silence succeeded the braying unison, and in this silence, Nectan strode to the center of the enclosure.

"Men of the Boar!" Loudly his voice rang out. "You have mustered at my command to witness the test of strength and courage that a Chief of the Boar must undergo every seventh year of his reign. It is our custom and law that this should be so. And it is our custom and law that a Chief who fails this test is no longer fit to be your Chief. Do any of you challenge this?"

"I challenge you, Nectan! I challenge you to tell us why you have so suddenly decided to undergo this test when it is only five years since you last endured it!"

Fand and Coll glanced at one another. The voice came from the part of the enclosure opposite the dais, and the warrior ranks there were crowded too closely for them to be able to see who had called out. But the voice had small peculiarities of accent that left no doubt about the identity of its owner. Taran had shown that he was at least ready to be drawn into the open, Coll thought, and waited tensely to see how Nectan would answer the challenge. He had turned toward its sound, and now his voice came powerfully, arrogantly.

"Does any Chief of the Boar need to give reasons for putting his life willingly at stake?"

It was the perfect answer, the only one acceptable to a tribe that worshiped courage—the answer of a hero! Coll cheered, leading the roar of applause it brought from every aspect of the enclosure. Nectan allowed the tumult to grow briefly, then he wheeled toward the trumpeters. His upraised hand stilled the roaring voices. The trumpeters sounded their braying notes again. The figure of Anu appeared suddenly among them. The trumpets spoke yet again, and Anu moved forward into the enclosure.

Slow, she moved, with infinite grace in every line of her tall form. Her long woolen cloak floated loose from her shoulders, the fringe of gold at its hem sweeping the ground, its swaying folds opening to display the gold thread outlining each scarlet and purple square in its checkered design.

Gold gleamed from her also in the bracelets clasping her arms, and her necklace of twisted strands of gold. Her tunic of scarlet wool was richly embroidered with gold thread. Her hair had been dyed a pale straw-gold for the occasion, and she wore it piled high in three braids pinned with golden combs, with a fourth tress streaming free and glittering over her shoulders.

Her slow step brought her level with Nectan, and she passed him by without a word or a glance in his direction. On she came, to the dais where Coll waited with Fand and Clodha, and staring in fascination at her approach, Coll found it impossible to think of her now only as Anu, the wife of Nectan and mother of Nectan's children.

This Anu was the mother of them all—a goddess mother! And the goddess had chosen Nectan to protect her tribe, her children; chosen him also to give her daughters to carry on her line and be mothers, in their turn, to the people of the Boar!

She was close to the dais now. With bowed, respectful

heads, the warriors standing in front of it parted their ranks for her. She passed by Coll and Fand to mount to the upper platform, and with a little shock of sympathy then, Coll noticed that she was very pale under the cosmetic blush on her cheeks and that she was holding her reddened fingernails clenched tight against the skin of her palms. Yet it was still she who would have to give the signal for the test; and if Nectan failed in it, it was she who would have to cry finish to twenty years of marriage and cast him out from his position as Chief!

Fand was shivering. With a gentle pressure of one arm across her shoulders, he steadied her, and glanced up toward Anu. She and Clodha were standing side by side now. Clodha, he noticed, was also pale, and it flashed across his mind that she would be someday in Anu's place. Someday she would have to give the signal that might bring death or dishonor to Niall, as Anu was about to give the signal that might bring death or dishonor to Nectan.

Anu raised one hand, and immediately the warriors massed against the enclosure wall stood close in three ranks. The front rank knelt with their shields held close to their bodies and rigidly upright. The second rank knelt also, alternating in position with the men of the front rank and advancing their shields so that each one overlapped the adjacent edges of the two in front of it. The third rank of men stood close behind the second rank, each man interposing his shield between his own body and that of the man in front.

Now there was a strongly woven fence of metaled men surrounding the open space at the center of the enclosure. Nectan moved to position himself carefully a little off-center of this space, and stood there as motionless as a bronze statue of a man. Anu held up her other hand. The trumpeters raised their instruments, and three times sounded their long, braying notes.

Outside the enclosure two men, who had been waiting for the last of these notes, raised the gate of an animal pen. Something moved, a blur of something dark flashing past the guardians of the pen, and became a wild boar racing into the enclosure.

It was a creature in the prime of its strength, hump-necked, deep-chested, with lean flanks tapering to narrow, muscular hindquarters, and gleaming white tusks projected like twin sabers from its snout. Two hundred and fifty pounds of bone and muscle on the hoof—but the sunlight had momentarily blinded it, and Nectan was not directly in its path. It rushed past him, and the wall of shields at the far side of the enclosure took the impact of its charge.

The wall shivered. The crowd roared. Coll raised a hand quickly to check the scream of fear that broke from Fand, and was aware of Clodha also stifling a scream. Only Anu stood silent and motionless, as the boar squealed and pivoted to charge again.

It was this quick pivot, combined with its weight and speed, that made it so dangerous; and now, Coll realized, it could see the man standing solitary in its path. Holding his breath, he watched it hurtle toward Nectan.

The timing of Nectan's defense was split-second. Rising like a dancer on the balls of his feet, he made a whirling movement that spun his body out of the line of impact—yet still not quite far enough out. All around the enclosure, as the boar jerked to a stop, there was a quick intake of breath at the line of blood starting out on Nectan's left thigh. First strike to the boar! And now it was wheeling, lightning-quick, for a fresh charge.

Squealing, it rushed on Nectan, and he leaped high in the air, leapfrogging over it and pivoting on his landing to face it completing an identical turning movement. His knife hand flashed out and downward, and his body followed the arm's downward thrust in a rolling somersault that took him past the boar.

It wheeled again, plunging after him, and its tusks struck the ground where he had been a moment before. Blood streamed down its mask, dripping bright red over the whiteness of one gleaming tusk, and Coll found himself hugging Fand and yelling madly as he realized that Nectan's knife thrust had blinded the boar in its left eye.

It was charging him again, in one quick, short rush after another, and its speed had not slackened. But now Nectan was taking advantage of its blind side to dodge the rushes, and his knife hand was always ready. The boar brushed his legs as he twitched his body aside from one rush. The bright blade flashed along its left flank, and the enclosure erupted into cheering at the blood breaking from the long line of the wound.

Anu was weeping now. She stood as motionless as before, but the quick glance Coll shot at her showed the tears making little runnels through the red cosmetic on her cheeks. And Fand was no longer watching the struggle between man and beast. She stood with her eyes tightly closed, and it was only his supporting arm now that held her upright and apparently still a spectator. But Clodha—! Clodha was yelling as furiously as any of the men in the enclosure, her mouth wide open, her cheeks scarlet without the need of any cosmetic!

Coll spared one passing glance of fascination for her before his gaze switched back to the enclosure, for now was the high point of danger for Nectan there—now when the boar was maddened beyond endurance by the pain of its wounds.

It was bleeding freely, he saw, but although the loss of blood had taken some of the speed out of its charging, it had not subdued the fury of its anger. And Nectan was tiring! *"He is no longer a young man,"* Fand had said; and that was showing now in the slowing of his movements.

He leapfrogged the boar again, repeating his original defense against it; but this time he landed with a stumble, and the boar was on him before he could complete his turn to face it. He dropped to one knee, throwing his body sideways, but the move was only partly successful. The boar's right tusk ripped along his ribs, and with a gasping shout of pain he rolled over and onto his feet again.

"Finish it! Finish it quickly!" Coll yelled, knowing what every man there knew, what Nectan above all knew now—that with such a wound, it was now or never for him. But Nectan was keeping calm, ignoring all the useless, shouted advice coming to him from every part of the enclosure. He was circling, dodging, feinting away again from the boar's rushes, and still managing somehow to keep on its blind side. And now also, for some reason of his own, he was holding his knife between his teeth and facing the creature with bare hands.

Once more the boar brushed his legs as he twitched his body aside from one of its rushes; but this time, instead of striking at it, he threw himself down and forward so that his body landed along the full length of the boar's back. His reaching hands fastened on its tusks. Hauling back on them, forcing the snouted head painfully back and up, he was carried along in a wild, bumping rush. Then, in a squealing, shouting, plunging flurry, boar and man crashed together to the ground.

Coll had an explosive vision of Nectan's legs thrashing wildly about, of gleaming tusks gouging the air, of a bristled back heaving up and suddenly subsiding again. Then slowly the tangle of man and animal dissolved into the sight of Nectan staggering to his feet, and the boar's body lying inert with its throat slashed open and its head resting in a pool of blood.

Nectan was covered with blood, his own and the boar's. He stood there panting, his chest heaving, eyes fixed unseeingly on the knife in his hand. Then, as the wave of cheering in the enclosure broke on his ears, he turned slowly toward the dais where Anu stood. But Anu was already coming down from the dais, blindly thrusting her way through the warriors at its foot to run toward him, and swinging off her checkered cloak as she ran.

She reached his side and, breathless between tears and laughter, threw the gold and purple and scarlet of the cloak around him. He looked at her, then with a slow smile of triumph spreading over his face, handed her the bloodstained knife. Anu bent toward the dead boar and sketched the gesture of hacking off its head; and from the ranks of warriors surging all around came a rush of volunteers to make a reality of the ritual gesture.

Neith, fleet-footed Neith the hunter, was in the van of the rush. With two swift blows he severed the head, and with a triumphant yell that was echoed on all sides, raised it high on the point of his sword. Nectan clutched Anu's cloak to himself with one hand.

"Come!" he told her and, with his other arm around her shoulders, moved with her to the dais. Neith followed, with the boar's head still held high on his sword point, and the whole shouting, jostling throng of warriors fell into triumphant procession behind him.

Fand had disengaged herself from Coll's arm at the moment Anu left the dais, and now she and Clodha were standing side by side on its lower step, eagerly watching Nectan's approach. He halted in front of them, and smiled a little as he noted the relieved expression on Fand's face. But it was on Clodha that his eye finally rested, and it was to Clodha he said,

"I have given daughters to Anu, and Anu's blood will rule."

He moved past them, toward the upper step of the dais, and Coll saw the blood from his wounded side seeping through the folds of the cloak. In dismay he began,

"Your wounds, Nectan—"

"Will speak for me," Nectan interrupted sharply, and turned to face the wild excitement of the crowd around the dais.

"I have fought the boar!" Loudly his voice rang out over the confusion of other voices. "And I have won the victory! Therefore have I proved my courage, and upheld my right to be your Chief. Is that not so, Men of the Boar?"

A roar of affirmation answered him. Nectan waited till he could be heard above the din, then shouted,

"And you, for your part, are bound to follow all my decisions. Is *that* not so, Men of the Boar?"

Once again the crowd roared, with a volume that made their previous response sound like a murmur by comparison; and with an almost unbearable pounding of excitement at his heart, Coll realized that now was the moment Nectan had faced death to achieve. This frenzied crowd was all his now, to do with as he willed, and Nectan knew it! He was gathering himself for his final demand on their loyalty—but where was Taran in all this? Coll's gaze roamed frantically over the blur of faces in front of him as Nectan's voice rang out again,

"Then hear this decision! The Druid Domnall disputes my policy over the slave raiders, but I say that my policy must prevail. I defy Domnall! And I defy the curse he threatens to lay on me!"

With a fierce gesture Nectan threw aside the cloak covering his blood-smeared body. "I defy him for your sake, my people, for the good of this tribe. See how I have proved myself in blood to you, and doubt me if you dare! But even so, if your spirit is too weak to support me in this, I give you my assurance that you need not fear the Druid, for even he could not summon the magic to curse a whole tribe! And so answer me now, Men of the Boar. Will you follow Domnall? *Or will you follow me?*"

The vibrations of Nectan's voice were still hanging on the air as the crowd gave him its answer. With spears and swords flashing aloft, they roared his name like a battle cry. The roaring sound soared into a delirium of cheering. The ranks of the crowd heaved and churned as men stamped in time to their own yells. Those in the rear ranks surged forward to be nearer Nectan. Those already near him struggled with one another to touch his hands, his cloak, his feet—any part of his person their eager hands could reach.

He was like a god to them at that moment, Coll realized; but a god they were in danger of overwhelming with their worship. And his womenfolk also were in danger of being trampled underfoot in this turmoil! Urgently Coll signaled to Neith, still holding the dripping boar's head up at arm's length. Neith caught the meaning of the gesture and, with a wide sweep of his arm, tossed the head far out over the crowd.

The farther ranks scattered, yelling in triumphant pursuit of the trophy. A wild game of tossing the head from spear point to spear point developed, and as more and more men joined the sport, the pressure around the dais was eased.

Nectan sat down wearily on the upper step, his face gray now with loss of blood and the fierce drain on his emotions. Anu appeared with the herb woman, and kneeling on either side of him, the two women began dressing his wounds. The Council of Elders closed in around the dais. The mass of the crowd behind them thinned still further as men drifted from the enclosure to search for further diversion in the settlement beyond.

Taran must appear now, Coll reasoned, or else yield the victory entirely to Nectan; and once more he searched for Taran among the faces near him.

"I doubt if you have acted wisely in this, Nectan."

Conamaill, the oldest member of the Council, spoke over the heads of Anu and the herb woman; and wincing from the smart of the ointment they were smearing over his wounds, Nectan answered wryly,

"I acted in the only way open to my honor as Chief of

85

the Boar. And all those cheers you heard were the proof of that, Conamaill."

Conamaill shrugged. "We are elected men, of course," he acknowledged, "and so we cannot go against the spoken wish of the whole tribe. But—"

"Wise or unwise, Nectan has *my* support!" The Councillor called Dargart interrupted harshly, hunching powerful shoulders that had seen many battles and scowling aggressively at his fellow Councillors. Nectan turned from him and Conamaill, and looked toward another Councillor—a grave-faced man of his own age.

"Gartnait," he appealed. "You always speak sensibly. What have *you* to say now?"

Gartnait considered, then spoke in his usual dry, incisive manner. "It is dangerous to go against the Druid, but the tribe has no future otherwise. I stand with you, Nectan."

"And you, Niall. And you, Ogham . . ." Nectan's look traveled around the rest of the Councillors, and he named them severally. "Do you also stand with me?"

There was a nodding of heads and a general mutter of assent to his question, but the mutter was silenced abruptly by the Councillor called Ogham.

"I am against Nectan in this," he said quietly, "for Domnall has declared resistance to the raiders to be a matter of faith. And so Nectan challenges the gods when he challenges Domnall with this defiance."

It was Ogham who had found Bran in that long-ago time after the first raid, Coll remembered. And in some ways since then he had been a man apart—almost as if some of the mystery about Bran had touched him also. He looked at the thin, sad-eyed face opposing Nectan, and wondered what strange thoughts lay behind it now.

And Nectan, it seemed, was also wondering; for, biting his lip, he invited,

"Go on, Ogham. That is not all you have to say."

The mournful eyes studied Nectan for a moment, then with a sigh, Ogham agreed, "No, it is not; for thirteen years ago I held the child of destiny, Bran, in my arms, and heard the Druid seer Broichan prophesy that his fate was linked with ours. Our fate is therefore fixed, as Bran's fate is fixed, and nothing you can do will alter that. The gods have decreed it, and Domnall is the servant of the gods. They speak through him, and so to defy him is simply to defy our own inevitable fate."

"I respect your views, Ogham." Nectan answered without bitterness or anger, although his tone was hard. "But you must keep them to yourself, now that the die is cast. Remember that you are in a minority of one."

"He is *not* the only one to disagree with you!"

The voice addressing Nectan came suddenly and harshly from behind Ogham, and all the Councillors turned to stare in that direction. Ogham stepped hastily aside, and Taran came swaggering forward to take his place. The Council redirected its stare toward Nectan; and none of them, Coll thought, could have guessed that Nectan had deliberately played for just such a challenge. He was scowling with all the outrage the Council expected of him, and there was tightly controlled anger in his voice as he told Taran,

"You have neither the right nor the privilege to address this Council."

Taran shrugged. "I am aware of that," he answered coolly, "but what I have to say is too urgent to yield to right, and too important to wait on privilege."

There was a murmur of indignation among the Council at the insolence of this speech, and there was no pretense in Nectan's anger this time as he answered harshly,

"I will be the judge of that. And be warned. If you have broken the custom without good cause, you will suffer for it. Now say what you have to say, and be brief about it."

"Very well." Taran squared himself as if for battle, and looked Nectan straight in the eye. "Briefly, there is no need for your defiance of Domnall. We can combat the raiders as he commands, with the help of an alliance I have made for the Boar with the tribes of the Raven and the Deer."

A concerted gasp of surprise broke from the Council members, and Conamaill exclaimed angrily,

"*You* have made an alliance? You? You have no authority in this tribe!"

"That is beside the point now," Taran retorted. "All that matters at this moment is that Arcon and Deva have agreed to the alliance."

Conamaill was about to make angry contradiction of this; but having drawn Taran to challenge him, Nectan had every intention of meeting the challenge in his own way.

"And tell me," he interposed smoothly, "just how will this alliance help us to combat the raiders?"

"We will use watch fires instead of a trumpet sound to warn of the raiders' coming," Taran told him. "The smoke of these fires will be visible in the settlements of the Raven and the Deer, and will be a signal to them to muster in arms. Then, while we draw the raiders away from the beaches by appearing to fly before them, the Raven and the Deer will circle in from the right and from the left to cut them off from their boats. Thus, when the moment comes for us to turn and fight, we can fall on them with the combined strength of all three tribes, and destroy them utterly."

A silence followed while Nectan looked inquiringly around the Council members. "Well?" he invited at last. "I give you all leave to speak to this—neat—plan."

There was only a hint of irony in the way he hesitated over the word "neat," but Conamaill snapped up the suggestion in it and said derisively,

"A stupid plan! Raven and Deer have always been our enemies. And if we fly inland, what is there to prevent them attacking us instead of circling to attack the raiders?"

"Land," Taran answered. "That will be their benefit from the treaty. They want some of the fertile coastland that belongs to us. And how will they get that by breaking the terms of the alliance?"

"By combining against us, of course," Conamaill retorted, and Niall added,

"Something we have always striven to prevent in past times; for together, they are stronger than we are."

That was the very point Niall had made to Bran, Coll remembered, then heard Dargart chiming in,

"I will not fight alongside these small men with their old-fashioned swords and their magical poisoned arrows! I am a warrior—not a companion of witches!"

"You make fears out of your own foolish fancies, Dargart," Gartnait remarked coldly. "But it is still the case that any plan which calls for trust in such long-standing enemies is flawed from the start. Therefore, I am against this one."

"We will vote on it." Nectan held up a hand to forestall further discussion. "And quickly, since you are all aware of the arguments for and against it, and I am still losing blood."

"Then hear me," Ogham said instantly. "Taran's plan means we will not need to go against Domnall. And so I am for it."

Four other heads nodded reluctant agreement with this, but Conamaill shouted "Against!" and the rest of the Council echoed his shout. Nectan waited till the clamor had died, then, glancing around the Council members, he announced,

"And for all the reasons already given, I also am against 'this plan.' Thus, from a total vote of thirteen, five are for it, and eight are against."

Once again that was that deliberate hint of irony in the way he underlined "this plan"; and watching the flush that started out on Taran's face, Coll saw in it the dawning realization that Nectan had been confident from the start about the outcome of the vote.

Nectan's glance also lingered on Taran's mortified expression, and slowly beginning to rise, he continued,

"But there is something yet I would like to know; and that is the answer to a question which was raised earlier in this discussion and which was passed over then."

Fully erect now, and with the level of the dais step giving his blood-spattered, bandaged form a towering height over Taran, he demanded,

"Who gave *you* authority to speak for the tribe of the Boar? Answer me that, Taran. By whose authority was this alliance planned?"

Taran stared, with hatred blazing in his eyes, at the

grim face poised above him. His lips drew back in a rictus of anger, and through clenched teeth he ground out,

"I spoke with an authority greater than yours—with the authority of *Domnall*! And so count your Council's votes again, Nectan. Count them carefully, for Domnall will shortly be here to make his own count. And if your second count does not run in my favor, you will have more to fear than the threat of his magic. A great deal more!"

6
Despair

A raven, the bird of death, had flown ahead of them as they moved back to the dun, and that was evil omen enough. But when the raven perched on the sloping thatch of the roof and was joined there by another of its kind, Dargart had sent hastily for beer and announced his intention of getting drunk.

"If death is about for the Boar tonight," he declared, "I mean to do my share of living while I can!"

The other Councillors had joined him, in spite of Nectan's attempts at restraint, and as the hours slipped by without any sign of Domnall's appearance, the effects of strain began to be added to those of the beer. It was only Gartnait, Coll noticed, who had joined Nectan in keeping himself aloof from the drinking and the quarrelsome atmosphere that developed, and he was thankful that these two at least would be in a fit state to deal with Domnall when he finally did arrive.

He glanced at Fand, lying asleep with her head in Anu's lap. She was worn out by the events of the day and the anxiety of the long wait for Domnall, he realized, and was touched by the defenselessness of her sleeping face. Niall drew his attention with a hand on his arm, and said resentfully,

"Why does he keep us waiting? What does he hope to achieve by it?"

"See for yourself." Coll nodded around the faces in the dun. "These men are no longer fit to show a united front in argument against him. And as for the rest of the tribe . . ."

He stopped, turning his face to the starry darkness framed by the doorway of the dun. Clodha moved to join them, and all three sat looking out into the night and listening to the sounds of celebration coming from the settlement.

"Out there," Coll said eventually, "they will all be so drunk by the time Domnall arrives that a clever man will find it easy to confuse their loyalties. And Domnall is clever."

"Nectan should have postponed the celebration!" Niall exclaimed; but Clodha shrugged and asked,

"How could he? The people *will* have their customs, and it is the custom to celebrate the killing of the boar. And quite apart from that, the men of the other settlements have to be given food and drink before they return to their own homes."

"Especially drink," Coll remarked wryly. "That is always the way with our people—one of our bad customs."

"Coll—" Niall hesitated, and then rushed on. "Domnall will not easily lose this struggle for power, and if he does win it Nectan would have no weapon at all left against him—unless you could persuade him to think again about your Stronghold."

Once more he hesitated, glancing at Nectan, and finished in a lower tone, "Have you tried to speak to him again about it?"

Coll shook his head. "What would be the point?" he asked. "You heard how firmly he rejected it the first time I spoke."

Niall made no answer, and they sat in silence after that, listening to the noise from outside the dun, and the snatches of conversation within it. Conamaill began grumbling that Taran should never have been allowed to address the Council meeting, and finished by asserting loudly,

"We should have killed him while we had the chance."

"*I* would have killed him if Nectan had given the word," Dargart maintained. "He must have been plotting with Domnall for months before he spoke to us; and it would have given me pleasure, I tell you, to kill anyone so treacherous."

"You speak foolishly, both of you." Gartnait looked up from the chessboard lying between himself and Nectan. "Taran is nothing more than a tool in Domnall's hands, and killing him would only have hardened Domnall's purpose."

"Which is to assert his authority in a matter that is for *me* to decide. Remember that!" Nectan looked up in his turn, to warn. "Remember that this struggle is no longer over policy, but over power, and you have rightly chosen to support my side of it."

Coll looked at Niall with a shrug that invited him to see how Nectan's words had stressed the present hopelessness of his own cause; then frowned, as Dargart heaved himself to his feet and drunkenly shouted,

"We are with you, Nectan!"

But Conamaill had also risen, and now he was hushing Dargart down, his face tense as he exclaimed,

"Listen! There is a different note to the sound out there! Something is happening, something—"

Everyone except Nectan was rising now, looking at everybody else, then all eyes turned to the figure of Drostan bursting through the doorway.

"The Druid, Nectan!" Breathless between excitement and haste, Drostan panted out his message. "Domnall is here!"

Nectan rose stiffly to his feet and looked around the faces waiting for his next move. "It is forbidden for a Druid to enter under a household roof," he reminded them. "We must go to him."

Bracing himself then for the test of further movement, he made for the door with a stride that ignored the continuing pain of his wounds. Coll and Niall joined the rush to follow him, and it was not until he was through the gateway in the surrounding wall of the dun that Coll realized he had not looked to see if the womenfolk had come with them. But by that time also, the full impact of the scene in the settlement had struck him, and not for anything could he tear his eyes from the fascination of it.

There were fires everywhere, it seemed—dozens of small campfires glowing in cones of gold among the dark huddle of houses; and standing apart in a solitary glory of scarlet and yellow leaping fiercely into the night, was the great celebration fire with the body of the boar slung high on a roasting spit above it.

A mass of figures loomed and shifted weirdly against the flames' shifting light; men, women, and children, all milling about like figures engaged in some confused sort of dance. From the weaving figures rose a meaningless blur of calling, laughing voices. Dogs barked somewhere among the human din. The lonely sound of a child crying pierced it briefly. And ominously, like a slow swell of thunder underlying its feverish excitement, came the sound of storm waves breaking on the beach below the settlement.

The wind from the sea was gusting furiously. With one arm raised to shelter his face from it, Coll watched the sparks it sent scattering from the celebration fire. The heart of the fire roared, licking up darkness with a hundred scarlet tongues and exposing the purpose behind the seeming confusion in the settlement.

The people were hurrying to converge on the rising ground where the celebration fire was built, Coll realized; and toward Domnall, haranguing a group of men clustered around him there. He looked around for Niall, but Niall and all the others had gone on, leaving him alone at the fringe of the settlement; and hurriedly, as he grasped this situation, Coll started forward to join the figures streaming toward Domnall.

Someone was shouting now—a man's voice rising drunkenly above the general din—"*Why should we not follow our Chief?*" and Domnall's answer came indistinctly through a blur of other voices supporting the questioner.

"Because he would have you run, rather than fight! Because only a coward would give such advice!"

A shout of laughter followed on Domnall's words. Coll heard the question and answer repeated as he pushed forward, and the good-humored scorn of the laughter growing with each repetition. Neith, the hunter, leaped into the flare of light surrounding Domnall. With one hand pointing to the blackened body of the boar, he yelled,

"And there hangs the proof of Nectan's 'cowardice'!"

The laughter broke out again, and rose into a cheer as Nectan appeared beside Domnall. Coll continued to push determinedly through the tangle of people in his path, and reached the position of vantage he sought in time to hear Nectan say,

"You ask me why we rejected the plan Taran put forward. I answer you simply that it was a bad plan. Moreover, Taran had no authority to make an alliance for this tribe, and we would have had to take on trust his claims about Arcon and Deva."

"They gave me no fair hearing!" Taran had pushed forward from somewhere near the fire, and was shouting now at Domnall. But Domnall ignored him and answered Nectan instead.

"Then let Arcon and Deva speak now on their own behalf!"

A mutter of the names ran from mouth to mouth among those near enough to hear Domnall's words. Men glanced at one another, seeking his meaning. The mutter spread, and became a buzz of speculation. Why should Domnall mention Arcon and Deva? What had they to do with his interruption of the celebration? The crowd grouped tighter, gathered nearer to the focus of attention, speculated more openly. Then suddenly there was a moment that stilled all questions.

Arcon and Deva stood by Domnall's side, and even to those nearest them, it seemed there was something magical about this appearance; for no one had seen their coming, no one had heard a whisper of sound from it. They were simply there, as if the smoke of the fire itself had

97

materialized into the forms of two cloaked figures standing silently beside the Druid.

Dark faces looked impassively out from under the hoods of the cloaks. Bright dark eyes stared at the now-almost-silent gathering of the Boar. There was a gleam of gold at Deva's throat. Arcon's cloak was hung to show the glint of the bronze sword by his side. Both men looked small, compared to Nectan and Domnall. And yet, Coll thought, there was still something frightening about them—a secret, self-contained look, that was like a hint of some deadly power lurking behind the stillness of those dark faces. . . .

Arcon began speaking, addressing himself to Nectan, and it was the old language of the islands he used; the language that only the elderly people of the Boar now fully understood. Coll focused all his hearing in an effort to follow the meaning of the slow, guttural sounds, and wondered at the back of his mind how many others of those within earshot could grasp what was being said.

He looked around, gradually identifying the members of the Council among the men nearest the fire; and from the strained attention on the faces of the younger Councillors, saw that they were having the same difficulty as himself. But the glances passing between Conamaill and Ogham showed that they were finding it easy to understand Arcon, and Domnall was watching these two closely, as if trying to judge the significance of their glances.

"—And therefore," Arcon's slow voice continued, "we of the Deer and the Raven agreed to meet with one another, and with this man, Taran—"

"Let us get to the point, Arcon!" With stumbling impatience as he forced his tongue to the unaccustomed use of the old language, Nectan interrupted Arcon's cautious opening speech. "Taran has already spoken to us of this alliance, and his words were that you have agreed to help us combat the raiders in return for some of our land."

"That was the bargain," Arcon agreed. "Your people keep the richest land of the islands for corn, yet still hunt over our poor grazing pastures. We want a better share of the islands."

"And weapons!" Deva spoke quickly, with a gleam of greed in his sideways glance at the long sword Nectan wore belted over his tunic. "If we are to face the iron swords of the Romans, we too must have iron swords."

"That was fairly spoken!" Abruptly recalling his wandering glance on the words *iron swords*, Domnall turned to Nectan. "All the terms of the alliance are fair, Nectan, and worthy of your agreement."

"Except for one thing." Nectan spoke in his own language now, although Domnall had used the old tongue, and his tones gained their accustomed authority with it as he continued, "Who gives the assurance that the Raven and the Deer will not turn those iron swords against *us?*"

"That question is all-important, Domnall, and we must have an answer to it." Gartnait's precise tones were followed by a murmured chorus of agreement from other members of the Council. Domnall turned furiously on them, but before he could speak, Taran shouted,

"These men do not express the feelings of the rest of the tribe! They are all Nectan's men—all hand-picked by him to speak as *he* wishes."

"And you speak like the stranger you are," Nectan

told him coldly. "These are all elected men, chosen to speak for the whole tribe."

"And who does Niall, your future son-in-law, speak for?" Taran jeered. "And Gartnait and Conamaill, your oldest and dearest friends—who do they speak for? And what about Dargart? There is a stupid man if ever I saw one—a lazy useless creature, fat, full of idle boasts and wind, whose only passions in life are beer and—"

"*And my Chief!*" With a bull-like roar that drowned the rest of Taran's words, Dargart sprang forward, a knife swinging high and wide in his right hand. But Dargart was drunk, Coll realized in dismay. And Taran's head was as clear as his wits were quick.

He met Dargart in mid-rush, his own knife drawn and held underhanded, his left hand striking up hard to deflect Dargart's right arm, his knife thrusting forward into Dargart's chest. The great body jerked, and crumpled. Then Dargart was sagging, with his own weight thrusting the knife ever deeper into his chest until he was impaled along the whole length of the blade.

Taran heaved, pushing Dargart away from him with one hand and jerking his knife free with the other. A spout of blood from the wound, a last dying moan from Dargart, and it was all over. Dargart was a limp, sprawling heap on the ground, and Taran was looking along the line of the bloody blade at Nectan.

"I fought fair—one man against one man," he said quickly. "And it was Dargart who attacked."

"Nevertheless, Dargart died with honor!"

Nectan flung the retort in a voice that snarled with rage; then, reaching for his sword, he demanded,

"But where was *your* honor when you went behind my back to Domnall?"

Taran backed a step from the vengeance so evidently facing him. But the bandage across Nectan's chest had made his threatening movement slow and clumsy, so that he was still fumbling to grip his weapon when Domnall moved quickly between him and Taran, and Gartnait achieved a restraining grip on his sword arm.

"Taran has pleaded self-defense and I uphold that plea," Domnall declared, and while Nectan hesitated before the apparent justice of this, Gartnait said urgently,

"Killing Taran will not solve our problems—remember, we agreed on that."

Domnall chimed in, "Remember also that Taran has accused you of packing the Council with your own men, and you have still to prove him wrong in that—prove that the Council does indeed speak for the whole tribe!"

Nectan's eyes grew wary. His hand slid from his sword hilt, and Domnall added, "Tell the people of the alliance, Nectan. It is their right to know the reason for the Council's decisions—as you are not slow to remind me when it suits you. Speak to the people now, and let us hear whether they support *this* decision!"

Gartnait drew Nectan toward him, whispering urgently. Nectan listened, nodding his head as if hearing confirmation of some idea of his own; then with a gesture that silenced Gartnait, he swung off his cloak and bent to spread it over Dargart's body. Straightening, he summoned Niall and Conamaill with a look, and as they moved to lift the dead man into the shadows beyond the fire, he told Domnall,

"This was a brave man, and he must have the funeral rites of a hero."

"It shall be so," Domnall assured him. "But note well,

before you take up my challenge to speak to your people, Nectan. Today you defied the curse I threatened on you and you gained their support in that defiance. Now, with this speech, you are given a chance to retract your defiance and to persuade them to do likewise."

Domnall paused, as if to let the significance of this point sink in. "A *last* chance," he stressed. "Do you understand that, Nectan? One last chance before I pronounce a doom on the whole people of the Boar."

Nectan stared wordlessly at him; then, turning on his heel, he moved a step or two higher on the mound holding the fire. The crowd had become impatient as they waited for some explanation of what had been happening, and a ragged cheer broke from them as Nectan came clearly into their view. A group of men somewhere among them started up a drunken rendering of the traditional victory chant of the Boar, but Nectan called for silence, and the voices dropped away into exclamations and muffled laughter.

"Later you may chant," Nectan shouted, "but just now there are matters to be explained to you. Why is Domnall here? And why also have the Chiefs of the Raven and the Deer appeared where no man of their tribes has ever before dared to set foot?"

"They smelled the boar roasting!" a ribald voice suggested, and as the laughter it provoked scattered derisively into the darkness, Coll saw scowls of anger settling on the faces of Arcon and Deva. But there was nothing at all to be read in Domnall's face as Nectan shouted over the laughter,

"No, it was something else they smelled. Land! And iron weapons! They have planned with Domnall and the stranger, Taran, to offer us an alliance against the slave raiders in return for some of our fertile lands and the kind of swords which we possess and they lack. And Domnall has come with them to hear your answer to that offer. Will you give it to him, then? Will you say whether you wish to arm our ancient enemies, and join with them in fighting the raiders?"

Nectan could not have made out a worse case for the alliance, Coll thought, and listened apprehensively to the storm of protest growing out of the crowd's first disbelieving murmur. Nor was Nectan making any attempt to quell this uproar. On the contrary, his very posture encouraged it, for with an effort of will that conquered the weakening effect of his wounds, he was still holding himself fiercely erect. And poised thus, straddle-legged on the mound, with hands on hips and chin defiantly outthrust, he seemed the very embodiment of the truculence in the crowd's noise.

A spear came hurtling out of the darkness. It flashed toward Deva, and as he ducked from it, it landed with its point stabbing into the heart of the fire. Flames and sparks burst upward. The crowd roared. Conamaill and Ogham sprang forward, their faces appalled at this outrage against the tribe's ancient tradition of *fir fer*—the code of fair play that debarred any group from attacking a single man.

"*Fir fer!*" they yelled. "*Fir fer!* Where is your honor?"

The rest of the Council milled about, adding their appeal to the shouts of the other two, and for a moment, only the figures of Nectan and Domnall stood rock-firm beside the fire. Then abruptly the confusion settled, and with some surprise Coll realized that Arcon and Deva were there still. They must be very sure of themselves to stand their ground in the face of that hostile demonstration, he thought uneasily, then saw Domnall raising his arms in a signal for silence. The noise from the crowd died still further, and Domnall's voice rolled powerfully over the fading sound,

"Will you seal your fate so completely, then, Men of the Boar?"

There was more yet to come. With muttering, shifting unease, the crowd recognized this as Domnall brought his arms to rest again and peered angrily from one half-seen face to another.

"Today," he accused, "all you who stand here chose to follow Nectan in his defiance of me. And now, when you are offered a way of cancelling that defiance, you show you wish to reject it. But now also, before you finally commit yourselves to this, learn from me the truth of what will happen if you scatter before the raiders; and by such a display of tameness, encourage the Roman might to overrun your islands."

Domnall paused, straightening himself and dismissing individual faces from his vision. Blindly his eyes searched the wild storm-darkness above him. His hands reached out, the fingers grasping and curling as if to pluck words from the air. Then slow and deep as a funeral chant intoned, his voice boomed out again,

"There will be a slaughter here of every single priest in the great College of Druids that honors you with its presence. For Rome, which is tolerant of all other religions, has outlawed the sacred rite of sacrifice that is central to *our* faith—yours and mine! Rome has put out word that the priests of this faith must die. And what will happen to you, people of the Boar, once your Druids are dead!"

Silence, the silence of shock, followed Domnall's question. The moan of the wind gusting in from the sea, the dull roar of the sea itself, the crackle of the fire ruddily framing Domnall's figure—all seemed suddenly, indecently loud in that frightened hush.

Coll saw the faces in the line of his vision staring openmouthed, and the color fly abruptly from that of Nectan. He felt the skin of his own face grow tight, as if his features had suddenly frozen into the expression they wore. Domnall spoke into the silence he had created, his tone quiet now, yet still by some trick of projection carrying to the farthest outskirts of the crowd.

"What will become of knowledge once the Druids are dead?" this new, quiet voice asked. "Who will there be to preserve the traditions and lore of your tribe, and to teach these to a future generation? Who will read the stars? Who will calculate the movements of the sun and the moon, and make calendars of them for you? Who will practice magic to confuse your enemies? Who will give a just answer to disputes with other tribes? Who, Men of the Boar, will stand between you and the danger from the gods of the Otherworld?"

There was no answer to any of these questions. There could be no answer, Domnall's glance said as it roved around the watching faces; yet relentlessly he continued,

"Who will make the sacrifices and read the omens? Who will there be to sing the courage of the men who die in battle? And who will conduct you into this Otherworld of the gods, and to the afterlife that awaits you there?"

There was pain in his voice now, and on his face a look of deep mourning that hollowed his cheeks and made deep, dark holes of his eye sockets. The hair on Coll's neck prickled as he stared at this skull-like face. A feeling of fierce yearning seized him as the keening voice cried out again,

"For this is the burden of our faith, is it not? There *is* an Otherworld where you will live again—a world of eternal sunshine and unending music, of laughter and brave deeds and love and feasting; a world of gods and heroes. *But we Druids hold the key to the Otherworld!* You cannot enter it until we unlock its mysteries for you; and so this, above all, is what you will lose if the Romans overrun your land and destroy us!"

The edge of pain in Domnall's voice sharpened to the point of agony. The death's-head face convulsed as a final cry burst from him,

"Is that what you want, Men of the Boar?"

A murmur broke the silence holding the crowd, a murmur of many dissenting voices; but pitching his voice above the murmur's growing volume, Domnall shouted,

"To lose the key to the life beyond mortal death—is that what you want? To die as beasts die, without ceremony or sacrifice, or grave goods to take with you into the Otherworld; to die and stay forever a cold and eyeless body rotting in the earth—is *that* what you want?"

The murmur could not be contained now. It burst suddenly into a roar of dissent, and Coll found himself shouting along with the rest with a passion that made him momentarily hate Nectan. For Nectan was not shouting. The expression of shock had faded from his face and he was staring in tight-lipped fury at the Druid. And Domnall was staring at him, confronting him eye to eye, with an equal fury.

The long folds of his robe swayed in the gusting wind

as he raised his arms again to quell the voices of the crowd, and still keeping his eyes on Nectan as their clamor died, he shouted,

"Then hear me one last time, Men of the Boar, for Nectan has told you that not even I have magic enough to curse each life in a whole tribe. But I need no magic to force your obedience to me! I need only my authority as Chief Druid to pronounce this doom on any man who continues to defy me."

Nectan moved suddenly, half turning from Domnall as if he could no longer endure the steady confrontation of his eyes. Domnall moved also, one hand dropping down to his side as he swung to face the crowd. Then, with the index finger of his other hand pointing in a great sweep around the dim mass of their faces, he cried,

"I, Domnall, who speaks for the gods, will bar that man from their favor. I, Domnall, will refuse that man the rites of sacrifice. I, Domnall, will keep the door of the Otherworld locked against him. Thus, when his fleshly body dies, there will be no share for him in the afterlife. And this doom is pronounced for all time."

A moment of vast, enfolding silence followed the last note of Domnall's voice, and Coll felt his throat constricting with the horror of that moment. His sight blurred. His mind shrieked denial of the wild visions propelling themselves through it . . . *a face—his father's face, battered and bloody in the sand . . . people running, screaming, falling . . . the stiffly folded hands of a warrior corpse in a stone-lined grave. . . .*

A man could endure such visions of death when all his tradition and teaching assured him that death was not the end of life. But where now was the comfort in all those fireside tales of endless life in the Otherworld? Where now was the assurance that came from a lifetime of omens noted, of ritual observed, of sacrifice offered?

"*Lost!*" Coll thought wildly. The peace beyond the noise of terror, the hope, the joy, the fulfillment, the beckoning glory of that Otherworld—all were lost to them now through their defiance of Domnall. Now death *was* final, a cold quiet ending to everything. . . .

A whirling darkness took possession of Coll's mind, churning his thoughts, stupefying his brain. Then from somewhere far off, it seemed, he heard the wail of many voices calling an agonized protest; and vaguely, through the numbness that gripped him, he was aware of his own voice mingling with them.

Figures moved before his sight again, slowly, like figures in some time-distorted dream. He saw Nectan crumple and sink down on one knee, the pride that had defeated his pain apparently no longer able to hold him erect. The Council members began surging toward Domnall. Hands stretched beseechingly out of the crowd. Arcon drew his bronze sword and held it at arm's length —all in this same slow, dreamlike way.

Conamaill cried, "We yield, Domnall! We truly repent us, and we yield!"

Coll saw his hand come slowly, slowly out to touch the blade of Arcon's sword, and heard his voice crying high and distant like a voice carrying over wide wastes of sea. Then, as the hands of the Council came out one by one to touch the sword, as their voices cried one by one, *"We yield, and we truly repent us!"* Coll found his sight and hearing returning to normal again and woke fully to the fact that he was once more shouting in concert with the crowd.

It was Conamaill's cry of submission they had all taken up, he realized, and trembled with the thought that Domnall might not accept it. Anu had appeared, he saw, and was kneeling beside Nectan. Her face, upturned to Domnall, bore a terrible distortion of fear and rage; and for a wild moment it seemed to Coll that she meant to leap up and defy him in Nectan's place. But it was Nectan who had led them all to this point, Nectan who had placed them under the shadow of perpetual doom!

In panic fear of Anu's intentions, Coll shouted louder than ever. Taran stepped forward, the last of those to lay his hand on the bronze sword; then Arcon held the sword upright before his face, kissed the blade, and handed the sword to Domnall. Nectan lifted his bowed head, his eyes rested on the sword in Domnall's grasp, and slowly he began to rise.

Domnall held the sword upright, at arm's length from himself. Nectan moved toward it, his feet dragging, his face an empty, grimly set mask. He bent his head forward. The gleaming bronze of the sword dulled briefly where his stiff lips had touched it. Domnall lowered the blade so that it pointed toward Arcon and Deva, and turned to the crowd.

"So is the alliance sealed!" he shouted. "And so has this people returned to obedience to me! Therefore do I lift from you all the burden of the doom that was spoken."

Quickly he reversed the direction of the sword so that he was offering it, hilt first, to Arcon; and quickly, as Arcon took it from him, he stilled the ragged cheer that had greeted his announcement.

"But hear this, before you rejoice! You have angered

the gods, and repentance for that is not enough to regain their favor. There must be atonement also. A sacrifice must be made. And so prepare yourselves! Live cleanly, be obedient to the laws, honor the customs while I, the servant of the gods, consult the omens for the nature of that sacrifice and the time of its offering."

Imperiously then, he turned, his eyes sweeping past Nectan to rest on Taran; and Taran stepped forward in obedience to the command in his look. Domnall nodded from the sullen faces of the Council members, bunching fearfully away from him, to the slyly satisfied ones of Arcon and Deva.

"There are arrangements to be made," he said coldly, "details of the alliance to be discussed."

"There is also a place on the Council to be filled!" Taran faced about, with arrogant defiance in the stare he directed at the Council members. "And as the man who arranged this alliance, I claim the privilege of that place."

"Do any of you dispute this claim?" Domnall's voice broke the uneasy silence that followed; and it was Nectan, to Coll's astonishment, who answered,

"If we are to proceed with the alliance it is not privilege that permits Taran's election to the Council, but necessity that calls for it."

Taran turned toward Nectan. His voice and face sardonic, he remarked, "That was well observed! But I have one further claim to make, which is this. The tradition of this tribe commands that the man best fitted to protect the people shall succeed as Chief; and I claim to be that man, for this alliance will be the saving of the people. Therefore I demand now that your daughter, Clodha, be given to me in marriage."

"*I* shall never consent to such a marriage!" The voice was Anu's, shrilling out in a fury of denial, and cutting across it came the sound of Niall shouting. The ranks of the Councillors exploded into noisy confusion as he lunged forward to reach Taran and was held in check by some of the older men. Anu moved swiftly to confront Nectan, and bristling like a wildcat before him, she hissed,

"I have not bred daughters by you to this end, husband! This man does not care for the people. He cares only for power. And you must tell him that no daughter of *my* noble line will ever raise him to that power!"

Nectan heard her without any change in the expressionless mask of his face, then spoke low in reply—so low that no one but Anu heard his words. She nodded, as if accepting them, and he turned to call to the Council members,

"The boast Taran has made is not proved until the alliance itself is proved. That is my answer to this second claim. And now let us hear what you have to say to both his claims, for he can neither be elected to the Council, nor can he marry Clodha, unless you also give your consent."

Nectan was still fighting, Coll realized with surprise. Defeated, exhausted, he was still planning—what? Coll posed himself the question; and like a light flashing suddenly into the dark corners of his mind, came understanding of Nectan's strategy.

The election of Taran was an empty gesture, for Nectan would certainly exclude him from any secrets in the deliberations of the Council! As for Nectan's reply to the claim on Clodha, that was simply a bold attempt to gain time—and with time in hand they would at least be able to think beyond their present circumstances.

But would the Council members realize this? Would they see, as Nectan had done, that the very speed of Taran's bid for power had caused him to overreach himself? Hope flared unexpectedly in Coll's mind as he watched the Councillors' faces and told himself that there might yet be a way out of the situation Domnall had forced on them all.

The fire was dying now, and the storm building up over the sea was driving a scatter of fat raindrops against it. Now also, it was hardly possible to see the watching crowd of tribespeople, but he could hear the murmur of their voices mingling with the deeper sounds of the sea wind and the surf breaking on the beach.

The Council members had their heads together, whispering. The dying firelight threw random flickers over their features, so that a cheekbone, a nose, the gleam of an eye, were suddenly highlighted in the patternless shadow of the grouped faces. Domnall's face was also in shadow, but the last gleams of the fire threw Taran's features into bold relief, and he leaned toward the Council with a face that had the beakily intent look of a bird of prey about it.

"Have you decided?" The shadowed mask that was Domnall spoke impatiently. The group of Councillors looked toward him, then broke apart. Conamaill took a step forward.

"We agree with Nectan," he answered firmly. "It is necessary for us to accept Taran into the Council now; but he can make no claim on Clodha until he has proved his boast by the success of the alliance."

There was a moment's pause, then Domnall's voice came harsh and heavy out of the darkness. "So be it. Taran is justly answered. But remember this, and be warned. I am the Keeper of the laws and customs to which he has appealed, and when time has proved his right to claim Clodha, *I shall be there to uphold that claim!*"

There was no mistaking the finality of the threat in the last words. Coll's gleam of hope died as he heard them, and he asked himself why Nectan had bothered to fight this small delaying action. Taran would win in the end—he was bound to, for that was how Domnall willed it. And they were all completely at Domnall's mercy now!

7
Decisions

Nectan and Coll stepped through the gateway in the defense wall of the dun and paused to look out over the settlement. Nectan spoke, with his eyes resting on the blackened patch of ground where the celebration fire had burned a week before.

"Did you tell anyone I wanted to speak privately to you this morning?"

"Only Niall," Coll answered, and Nectan shrugged his indifference to this.

"Over there," he said, and pointed to a strip of smooth, sandy beach beyond the houses. "We can be more secret there than behind the thickest of walls."

Coll nodded agreement and bent to free two of the guard dogs lying beside the gateway. They would be added protection against any possibility of being overheard, he thought, and called them to heel as he followed Nectan along the path winding between the houses.

The sun of the late-April day was warm on them as

they walked, and Coll was aware of the peaceful, every-day activities of the settlement all around them. Life went on, he thought, in spite of the threat hanging over them all. There was still bread to be made, fishing nets to be mended. . . .

Echu, the smith, was hammering out a plowshare, and his son, Ibar, was carefully shaping a balk of driftwood into an ox yoke for the same plow. Women squatted by their doorways, bodies moving rhythmically as they fed grain into a quern with one hand and turned the grind-stone with the other. Men worked on the fishing nets strung between the houses, hands steadily performing the set pattern of movements for repairing the gaps in the mesh.

Left hand pulling the net taut, right hand darting up, over, and through, in the motions of the half hitch that drew each strand back to its place in the mesh. . . . Coll's glance traveled absently over the brown, lacy structure of the nets; and, as he often had before, he wondered what long-dead genius had invented the simple miracle of the half hitch. Then abruptly he was brought back to earth with the realization that the net menders were averting their eyes from Nectan.

A thrill of anger ran through him—unreasoning anger, he admitted, for it was small wonder the people were uneasy in Nectan's presence now. They had lost faith in his power to protect them on that night of the celebration fire, and it was fear of Domnall that had ruled them since then. Yet still the sullen looks, the averted eyes, rankled in his mind, and more than ever he tasted the bitterness of knowing that Nectan could no longer speak freely among his own people.

With angry loyalty he outfaced every stare that met his own, and when they finally halted at their objective, Nectan turned to smile at him.

"Now I know for certain I shall always be able to count on you, at least," he remarked. "But now also, I must discover if you are as clever as you are loyal. Tell me about your Stronghold, Coll."

"But why?" With surprise and doubt mingling in his mind, Coll stared at Nectan. "You would not listen to me the first time I spoke of it."

Nectan frowned. "Events have marched far beyond the point they were at then," he said impatiently. "Domnall has such a hold over us now that I *have* to come to terms with him. Moreover, Taran has come very near to replacing me as Chief. And all I have is the little time I have gained to decide what my next step should be."

Coll felt a sudden flush of resentment. All this could have been avoided, he thought, if only Nectan had not been so stubborn in the first place! With bitterness edging his tone, he asked,

"But it is too late for terms now, is it not? We are committed to Taran's plan."

"And you know the dangers of that as well as I do!" Nectan's answer flashed out with the same bitter edge to it. "The Raven and the Deer will prove treacherous, and so Taran's plan will fail. But when Anu married me, she placed the care of the people in my hands, and that is a task in which I cannot fail. I *must* find a way to cancel this foolish alliance. I *must* find some other way of obeying Domnall's command to stand and fight against the raiders."

"The safe way—the perfect defense against them . . ."

Coll murmured the words, half to himself, still trying to grasp that Nectan was at last convinced of the worth of his cherished idea; then realized he had taken too much for granted, as Nectan said briskly,

"Prove that to me!"

Elation shot through Coll, and with gleaming eyes he responded to the challenge. There were none of the flagstones that formed his usual building material on that part of the beach; but, he realized, there was a flat stretch of sand to draw on! Swiftly he knelt and used his forefinger to trace the ground plan of his Stronghold on its smooth, damp surface.

"Now," he told Nectan, "here is how I will build upon that plan."

With methodical care, then, he began another drawing that showed a cross section of the hollow wall with all its galleries. As he worked, he talked, explaining each stage of the building, and Nectan bent over him, carefully watching and listening. The drawing complete, Coll looked up, his face inviting comment, and Nectan said slowly,

"Let me be sure I have grasped this. Your method of building means that no scaffolding will be needed but the structure of the tower itself. Is that what you have been saying?"

Coll nodded. "Exactly that! And now for the way we will defend this Stronghold. First, the door—always the most vulnerable part of any defense structure ..."

Bending to the sand again, and with his forefinger rapidly tracing a series of rough illustrations on it, Coll launched into a detailed explanation of the tower's defenses. Nectan listened with only an occasional nod or mutter to interrupt the flow of his words; but there was a smile of grim pleasure on his face by the time Coll had finished, and his voice was rich with satisfaction as he said,

"There is no flaw, Coll. I can see no single flaw in anything you say. This Stronghold *is* a perfect defense!"

"Then you will let me build it?" Coll asked eagerly.

The smile faded from Nectan's face. "Not yet," he answered. "I must first consider how best to persuade Domnall to accept it in place of Taran's plan. And once that decision is made, it must be put to him with the support of as many of the Councillors as possible."

"But you cannot let Taran into any of your plans," Coll pointed out. "And that means you cannot call a Council meeting to discuss this."

"But Conamaill is of my household," Nectan reminded him, "and so he is always at hand to carry messages to the Councillors in other settlements. Moreover, I can trust him to speak always as I would speak, and to keep his visits secret from Taran."

"Ogham is also of your household," Coll ventured. "Will you trust him in this way too?"

"I think I know what is in your mind, Coll." Nectan darted a glance of shrewd understanding at him, and continued. "We are all, I hope, faithful to the gods. But the part that Ogham played in the prophecy concerning your brother has marked him strangely in some ways, and there are times when I think his devotion to the gods borders on lunacy. He might see a challenge to Domnall in this, instead of an attempt to come to terms with him, and he would look on that as a challenge to the gods themselves. It would be most unwise to tell him anything meantime."

"And Niall?" Hopefully Coll named the one remaining Councillor in Nectan's household. "You will let him into your confidence, surely?"

"No." Nectan's voice was firm. "I will not speak to Niall about this." He glanced at Coll with a smile suddenly twitching the corner of his mouth. "But *you* may do so!"

"Now?" Coll demanded.

Nectan sighed. "You young people—you are so impatient! What difference would now or tomorrow make?"

"None—except that I have already waited thirteen years for this moment!"

Coll threw his answer back over his shoulder as he started eagerly forward from Nectan's side. The hounds followed his move, taking it as permission for them to run also, and when he realized that Nectan did not intend to call them back, he whooped them on with him.

Limp or no limp, he told himself exultantly, he would race them along the beach to find Niall, and blessed the foresight which had led them to agree on a meeting after the conversation with Nectan. Niall, he remembered, had made all sorts of guesses at what Nectan might have to say, but it had never even occurred to him that the Stronghold was to be the subject of the talk!

The rocks of their private meeting place began looming up ahead, but now, in spite of all his efforts, the hounds were drawing well out in front of him. Wryly he watched their long gray forms streaking for the rocks, and waited for Niall to hear them and to emerge in greeting. But no one appeared from among the rocks, and suddenly, to his surprise, the hounds halted their headlong pace.

They had "found," Coll thought. He ran on, expecting

the game to break cover; but nothing happened, and now the hounds were snarling. It was human quarry they scented, he realized, then hallooed in alarm as the figure of Fand came into view.

"Down, Brecc! Down, Cumhal! *Down!*"

Yelling, he made a desperate spurt for the hounds leaping at Fand; and even while the rational part of his mind argued that they knew Fand, they would never attack her, he felt sick with horror as he saw her bowled over by their rush. She lay still where she fell, her body almost hidden by the two huge gray forms above her; then with a shock of relief, as he rushed to tear the creatures away, Coll heard her laughing.

The hounds were slobbering over her, whining, darting great tongues at her face, pawing the upraised hands she was using to fend off their caresses, and she was almost choking with laughter as she tried to rise again. Coll vented his relief in anger, fiercely cuffing the hounds into obedience and shouting at Fand,

"These are guard animals, not pets! If they snarled it was for some good reason, and you had no right to distract them from their duty."

Fand looked up at him, the laughter fading off her face; then, rising, she brushed the sand from her tunic and deliberately made a small ritual of retying the strip of plaited leather encircling her slender waist. This settled to her satisfaction, she drew herself up with a haughty air that was clearly imitated from Anu.

"There are times, Coll," she remarked, "when you go too far in your care of me. I am not stupid. I am no longer a child. *And I do not belong to you.* Please to remember all these things."

Coll felt himself flushing at her tone. She could copy Anu very well when it pleased her, he thought; for, despite her gentleness, she had a good share of her mother's highborn pride. But her features—that small straight nose and oval chin, that finely shaped upper lip and the generous lower one—would always be a delicately feminine version of Nectan's features. And when the blue of her eyes darkened so with anger, it was Nectan's eyes that looked out at him and Nectan's anger he saw!

"But the hounds—" he began awkwardly. "They were—"

"The hounds scented your brother." Sharply Fand interrupted Coll's attempt to justify himself. "That was why they snarled, and that was why I distracted them. Would you have preferred me to let them tear Bran to pieces?"

Coll stared in astonishment. "Bran is here?" he exclaimed. "You mean that he has shown face to you—without waiting for me to appear?"

"And why not?" Fand asked. "After all, we were here with you—Clodha and Niall and myself—the last time he came."

"Of course, of course." Coll nodded, and collected his scattered wits enough to remember the day after the celebration fire when Bran had come hotfoot to learn what had happened then. And after all, he told himself, this was what Bran had wanted—to meet the others and be part of their circle of friendship. He realized that Fand had begun to smile again, and was thankful their quarrel had been so brief. With a shrug that dismissed his surprise over Bran, he remarked,

"It seems he is not so shy as I thought he was."

Fand's smile broadened to a laugh. "He is not shy at

all," she declared. "He is wary—which is quite a different thing!"

"True," Coll agreed. "And who can blame him when he risks Domnall's anger to visit us?"

He moved forward, gripping the hounds as he did so. The gesture brought his race along the beach suddenly back to mind, and he turned to ask Fand,

"But where is Niall? I told him I would meet him here after I discovered what Nectan wanted of me."

Fand made a vague gesture seaward and told him, "Over there, at the edge of the rocks, looking at some lines he has set out. But he said to tell you he would not be away for long."

Coll could see Bran now, standing beside the pool in the sheltered place among the rocks, and the hounds were snarling again as they also sighted him. Coll soothed them into silence, and noticed as he did so that Clodha was seated some yards from Bran, her knees drawn up to her chin, and her face hidden in her hands.

"There is no use in speaking to her," Fand whispered. "She is still in such despair over Taran that even Niall cannot rouse her out of it."

Coll nodded understanding, and left the hounds in their customary guard position as he went forward to meet Bran. But Clodha was listening, it seemed, in spite of her withdrawn attitude, for her head jerked up at the sound of Bran's first words.

"I have some things to tell you, Coll—about Taran."

Bran paused to glance aside at Clodha, and told her gently, "And one of them may be of interest to you, if you care to make it so."

Clodha stared at him. She looked wretched, Coll

thought compassionately; her face pale and thin, her eyes deep-sunken and tormented by the past week's brooding over Taran's threat to her future with Niall. He watched her as she rose slowly, and spoke low to Bran,

"If you have anything to say to ease her misery—say it quickly!"

The pale face in its frame of golden hair remained unruffled by the urgency of his tone. The brilliant gray eyes looked levelly at him, then slid aside to Clodha. In the gentle tone he had used before, Bran asked her,

"Do you remember a carnelian? A talisman that Taran carried with him, and that he showed you on the day he tried to attack Coll with a knife?"

"I remember." A spark of interest came into Clodha's sullen face. "Taran said he could not be killed so long as he was carrying it."

"It was his good-luck piece," Fand chimed in. "And *you* knew about it because you were in hiding that day, listening to us talk."

Bran's self-mocking little smile flashed out at her, then his eyes came back to Coll. "Listen then," he said. "Taran came again to the Ring last night, to see Domnall, and I made an opportunity to speak to him. He was not guarded in his speech with me—perhaps because he thought me too young to be of any importance—and I learned a great deal from what he said. First of all, that his killing of Dargart was no accident—"

"He planned that?" Coll interrupted. "But how could he?"

"Because he knew it was almost certain that Dargart would be drunk that night," Bran said calmly. "He also knew that Dargart was a very touchy man, and so he deliberately provoked him into the attack that led to his death."

"And therefore to a vacant place on the Council!" Coll exclaimed.

Bran nodded. "Of course! Then he aimed for Nectan's position as Chief, through his claim to Clodha. But Domnall is mistaken in thinking that Taran has been his tool in all this, even though it was planned between them. Taran is deceiving Domnall as much as he has tried to deceive you, for he does not care for our gods. They mean nothing to a stranger like him, and he does not fear them—I could tell that by the way he behaved and spoke in the Ring last night. And when the time comes for *him* to defy Domnall, he will not be afraid to do so."

"But why should he defy Domnall," Coll demanded, "when he can achieve all he wants by working with the Druids?"

"How do you know how far Taran's ambitions go?" Bran asked quietly. "Supposing he is determined to rule the Raven and the Deer as well as the people of the Boar? The islands would be a power to be reckoned with then, united under the rule of one Chief—would they not? And could not such a Chief raid successfully on the mainland of Britain, and so even further extend his power? For this Taran is a man who naturally cares for power—you said so yourself, Coll—and now it is clear, to me at least, that *he cares for nothing else*! That is why I am certain his ambition will not stop at being Chief of the Boar."

"And the carnelian?" Clodha had been growing visibly more impatient all the time Bran had been talking, and now she continued quickly before Coll had a chance to say anything. "Why did you mention that?"

Bran's earnest expression changed suddenly to a grin of impudent delight. "Because I stole it from him! Like this—look!"

His right hand shot out in a closed fist, then opened to show the dark red of Taran's carnelian resting on his palm. The hand balled into a fist again, turned swiftly on a flexible wrist, then flipped open once more to present an empty palm to the three watching faces.

"You see?" Bran spoke across their gasps of astonishment. "That was finger magic! I learned it from Domnall. And last night I coaxed Taran into boasting about his carnelian, and asked to look at it. Then I used finger magic to steal it and put a pebble in its place, in that little bag Taran wears round his neck. I stole Taran's luck from him!"

"But why? Why did you do that?" Fand asked. She sounded breathless, and a little scared, and Bran looked in surprise at her.

"To frighten him, of course," he said impatiently. "A carnelian *is* a powerful talisman, remember, and Taran will not be nearly so sure of himself now that he no longer has this one to protect him."

"Bring it back," Clodha urged. "Bring it back from—from wherever the magic sent it."

Bran's delighted grin flashed out again. His hand made a grasping motion in the air, and opened to show the carnelian once more lying on his palm. Fand gasped and crowded forward for a closer look.

"That *was* magic!" she exclaimed, but Clodha spoke in the same breath, and her voice was harsh.

"*Give it to me!*"

Bran looked uncertainly at her. "If you wish—" he began, and Clodha interrupted,

"You said it might interest me, and it does. Give it to me!"

She reached out to snatch the stone, then held it up between thumb and forefinger. Bran shrank back from the gesture, and from the hatred blazing suddenly in the dark eyes fixed on the little spot of red. Clodha spoke without taking her gaze off the carnelian.

"I know another magic, Bran—a more powerful one than the game *you* played with this."

Dropping swiftly to one knee, she placed the carnelian on a rock, then picked up another rock and smashed it hard against the first one. The carnelian cracked under the impact of the blow, and she hit it again and again till there was nothing left of it but a little pinkish-brown patch of powder.

Clodha stared at the powdery patch, her shoulders heaving with the effort behind the savagery of her blows, her breath coming in gasps. The stone dropped from her grasp. She glanced up once, hatred still smoldering in her eyes; then with a little shivering sigh she brushed the remains of the carnelian away and rose to her feet.

The other three watched in silence as she moved away from them to stand gazing seaward, and it crossed Coll's mind that there was a great deal of her mother in Clodha. Anu would not shrink from killing a man if it were necessary; and Clodha's actions had been a ritual killing if ever he had seen one, for she had certainly wished a death magic on Taran as she destroyed the carnelian!

Bran said uneasily, "Will I go now? I have nothing more to tell you, and—"

"But you cannot go yet!" Fand interrupted. "We have not finished our game!"

She looked so comically disappointed that, in spite of the tension Clodha had created, Coll felt inclined to laugh.

"What game?" he questioned, and Fand pointed to a rock which had its flat surface marked out in squares, with pebbles set like counters in each of the squares.

"There," she told him, and moved to kneel beside the rock. "I am teaching Bran to play *fidchell*."

Deftly she put one of the pebble counters through a series of moves, then smiled a challenge up at Bran. He studied the positions on the makeshift board, smiling a little also as he told Coll wryly,

"And you can see how badly I am faring in the play!"

Fand laughed aloud at this. "He could still win, could he not?" she asked Coll, and anticipated his answer by telling Bran, "If you thought far enough ahead with *your* next move!"

"But you cheat," Bran protested. "You know you do! You tell me something is not in the rules, and then you make that very move with your own counters."

"I do *not* cheat," Fand argued. "I simply know the rules better than you do."

"If you know the rules you should keep to them," Bran told her. "That is what rules are for."

"And if you are going to be a bad loser," Fand retorted, "this is the last game I shall teach you."

"Coll . . ." Sighing in exasperation, Bran turned to appeal for support in his argument, but with a grin and a wave of his hand, Coll left them to their squabbling. They were perfectly happy at it, he decided. Fand was delighted to have someone younger than herself to bully, after having been so long the baby of their group; and as for Bran, he was making up at last for all the years of companionship he had missed. A few arguments would be good for both of them, and meanwhile, it was still important for him to find Niall.

Whistling to the hounds to follow him, he began working his way over the rocks toward the little bay where Niall was in the habit of setting his fishing lines; and saw the figure he sought, standing on the highest point of the rocks. Clodha came scrambling after him as he waved and shouted to attract Niall's attention. Niall called back, then pointed urgently westward to the settlement before starting to meet him; and turning in that direction, Coll saw a figure running fast along the beach toward them.

It was Ibar, the son of Echu the smith, he realized, recognizing the stride of the lanky young legs and the glint of the boy's red hair; and heard Clodha speaking at his elbow as she too identified the runner.

"And there must be something wrong at the settlement to account for *that*!" she added, for now they could also see what had caused Niall's urgent pointing. Ibar was carrying the boar's-head banner that showed he was Nectan's messenger.

His own news would have to keep for the moment, Coll realized, and waited anxiously for Niall to close the distance between them. He was leaping over the rocks, scrambling and slipping in his haste, and covering the last few yards between them, he panted,

"Move, Coll—run on to meet Ibar! And Clodha, warn Bran that he must—"

"Bran has gone." Fand came suddenly up behind them, interrupting Niall's instructions. "He heard the shouting and just rose and vanished, the way he always does if he thinks anyone but us might see him. And Coll—"

Niall started off without waiting for her to finish, dragging Clodha by the hand as he went. Coll hurried after them, and Fand stumbled alongside, clutching at his arm and stubbornly persisting,

"And Coll, before he left, he said something that frightened me. He said, *'So soon?'* Like that—like a question. And there was such a strange look in his eyes —as if he was seeing something I could not see. And then his face twisted as if he was about to weep, and he cried out, *'But I have not had time—not nearly enough time!'* "

Coll's eyes were on the figure of Ibar, now rapidly closing with them, and he only half heard the anxious voice at his side. He glanced down at Fand, nevertheless, and felt vaguely resentful of the alarm Bran had caused her.

"What did he mean, Coll? Why did he speak like that?" Fand held the harder to his arm as she asked her questions; but Ibar was too close now for any more time to be wasted on Bran.

"Probably nothing," he answered irritably. "You know how strange he can be."

None too gently, then, he freed himself from the clutching hand, and raced on. Ibar was shouting, and as Coll caught up with Niall to close the gap between them, Ibar's voice came clearly,

"Coll! Niall! You are to go at once to Nectan. At once!"

They met face to face with him, and Niall demanded, "What has happened, Ibar? Why has he sent for us?"

"He has had a message from Domnall," Ibar panted. "Broichan came with it—Broichan, the Druid seer. Nectan sent me running for you the moment he heard it."

Niall wasted no more time. "Bring the womenfolk back with you," he ordered Ibar, and glanced at Coll.

"I am with you," Coll responded, and moved simultaneously with him, away from the group. Their steps matched as Coll took up his familiar position, half a pace behind Niall with one hand on the other's shoulder. The hounds, that had meanwhile been prowling uneasily on the edge of all this activity, followed at heel, and moving steadily in this compact group, they thudded off along the beach.

The urgency of Ibar's message had blotted everything else from his mind, Coll found, and he ran in silence with no thought except keeping the pace Niall set. Niall had nothing to say either, and still without a word he led the way eventually through the flurry of men and dogs that greeted their arrival at the gate in the dun's defense wall.

The group of figures inside the dun itself faced toward their entrance there. In the shaft of light falling through the doorway, Coll briefly made out the faces of Nectan, Anu, Conamaill, and Ogham. Then Nectan spoke.

"You tell them, Conamaill. I cannot—cannot bring myself to say it."

"Must I?" Conamaill glanced pleadingly at Nectan. His face was drawn and pale, Coll noticed, and Anu was pale also. Nectan himself had a dazed look, but Ogham—! Frowning as his gaze traveled over Ogham's face, Coll realized that the look it bore was one of exaltation. His eyes shone like those of a man in the grip of fever, and even in the dimness of the dun's interior it was possible to see the glow that transfigured his features.

"For pity's sake, *somebody* speak!" Niall exploded.

Nectan turned his face away, and nervously trying to clear a hoarseness from his throat, Conamaill began,

"Domnall has sent a message to say that he has set a date for the atonement that must be made to the gods. It is to be at sunrise, seven days from now, on the festival of Beltane. And the gods have also named to him the sacrifice that must be made then."

The hoarse voice stumbled on the next word, and died; but Ogham's lips had been moving silently all the time Conamaill spoke; and now, like a man who could no longer contain his ecstasy in silence, he cried,

"Young, young and pure must be the sacrifice, a creature without stain or blemish; for only this is a fit offering to the gods! Only this can appease their anger, and bring us back into their favor! And the honor of becoming such a sacrifice has fallen on—"

"*Silence, you—you madman!*" Roaring, like a man sent berserk by the pain of a mortal wound, Nectan swung around to cut off the rest of Ogham's speech, and pantingly continued,

"This is no 'honor,' this cruel thing that has been done! Domnall is seeking to break me—to break me completely. And it is through my daughters he has chosen to do so—first, by promising the Chiefdom to my enemy, through Clodha—"

"Clodha! Is it she? Is she to be the sacrifice?"

Shouting, Niall lunged forward to grip hold of Nectan's shoulder. Nectan gaped at him, the anger fading off his face, the dazed look returning to it. Coll's heart leaped in a sudden terror of anticipation, and for an eternity of time, it seemed, he watched Nectan's lips working in an effort to speak. Then at last the words came; stumbling, whispered words.

"No—can you not see? There is only one way Domnall could lose control of the Boar now—if some determined man were to marry Fand, and rally the people around him in opposition to Taran. And so it is *she* who is to be the sacrifice—Fand—my little Fand...."

8
Victim

For three days, Fand had gone through the motions of living.

She moved, dressed herself and combed her hair, took a dish of food when it was offered, lay down on her bed at night and rose in the morning. But she did not eat, she seldom spoke, and whether the hours in her bed were spent in waking or sleeping, no one could tell. It was as if she were already dead, Coll thought; and this, her fragile little ghost, moved among them to remind them that she had once been Fand, and alive.

It was Anu who had broken the news to her. Nectan, who had had the courage to face the wild boar, had not been brave enough for that; and after the first bewilderment, after the first wild passion of protest, had come this silent shadow play of living. But it was with those first screams of protest still ringing in their ears that Coll and Niall had retreated from the scene between Anu and

Fand, and stumbling along at Niall's side, Coll said desperately,

"We must save her—we *must*!"

Niall looked at him in shocked uneasiness. "But no one can interfere with the Druids' choice of a sacrifice, Coll. That would be sacrilege!"

"You would not say that if Clodha had been chosen," Coll raged, and Niall turned a troubled face away.

"If it had been Clodha," he admitted, "I would have felt as you feel. But even so, what could I do? What can any man do against the will of the gods?"

"But how do you know this is the will of the gods?" Coll shouted. "Nectan does not think so—and you heard what he said to Ogham. Fand is to be killed to suit Taran's purpose!"

"That was only a guess on Nectan's part," Niall returned, and swiftly Coll retorted,

"Then it was a good guess, for today Bran told me that Taran visited Domnall after the night of the celebration fire. And why should he do that, if not for some further scheming to improve the position he achieved then? What better way could Domnall choose to help him destroy Nectan than by naming Fand for sacrifice?"

"Keep your voice down," Niall told him sharply, "or Nectan will be destroyed more surely than by any scheme of Domnall's."

With his own voice dropping to a whisper, he added, "You know it is blasphemy even to suggest that the Chief Druid would interpret the gods' command to suit himself. And the people would not risk further angering the gods if they knew Nectan held such a view. They would depose him, or even kill him, rather than run the danger of allowing him to remain their Chief."

"The first lesson of a Chief!" Coll jeered. "Hold on to power, whatever the cost. You are schooling yourself well to become Chief in your turn, Niall!"

"You have mistaken the lesson," Niall told him coldly. "Hold on to power for the good of the people—that is what it says. And even if Nectan does not yet see that he cannot destroy himself for the sake of Fand, Anu will soon convince him of that."

Coll stared at him. "But she loves Fand—they both love Fand. How can you talk like that?"

"Because I have had to learn those very lessons you scoff at," Niall snapped; "lessons about the duties of a Chief. And because we cannot be sure that Nectan is right about Domnall's motives—whatever Bran may have told you. But even if Bran is right, there is nothing we can do about Fand without being held guilty of sacrilege. And you know the punishment for that!"

The argument was going around in a circle, Coll realized in dismay, yet still could not help coming back to the attack.

"But you would risk that for Clodha. You would die for her, would you not?"

Niall looked at him for a long moment. "I would die—yes," he answered slowly. "But you are not thinking of what you are saying, Coll. The man who commits sacrilege dies cursed—banished forever from the gods and from the afterlife. Could I bring myself to suffer such a punishment, even for Clodha? I do not know. And so how could I bring myself to suffer it for Fand?"

Coll stared at him, silenced for the moment by the bleak honesty of the words. Then abruptly he turned his back on Niall, and strode away from him.

They had made for the beach when they escaped from

the dun, and now the receding tide had left the sand wet and soft underfoot. The women of the settlement were scattered over the rocks, gathering the shellfish left by the ebb and singing as they worked; but Coll had no eyes or ears for the women's presence, and he scarcely noticed the suck and drag of the sand on his progress.

If this was Niall's attitude, he asked himself, what could he expect from Anu? And from Nectan, once Anu had worked on his mind? And supposing Nectan *had* been wrong about Domnall's motives. Who could then dare to dispute the naming of Fand for sacrifice?

It was necessary, after all, for the earth to have pure young blood spilled on it at Beltane; for how otherwise could the crops that sprang from it and the beasts that fed on it be made fertile? How otherwise could the Druids summon the magic of Belenos, the summer god, to ensure that this would be so? And since the gods were angered, was it not only to be expected that the noblest blood of all should be necessary for this year's Beltane sacrifice?

Questions without answers spun through Coll's mind. Arguments without end engrossed him, and suddenly in memory he was once more in Nectan's dun, lying on the restless couch of his childhood injury. From niches set high in the interior walls of the dun, the heads of the gods regarded him; and his fevered glance was flickering over those stone heads, his heart was beating with the old terror of their eyeless stare.

There was Lugh, the god of harvest, winking one hollow socket at him and smiling grossly with bulging stone cheeks. The head of Ernunnos, the horned god of three faces, had his scowling face of war turned perpetually toward the interior of the dun. And there was Cromm, the god of evil, his head of black stone leering from the niche next to that of the Dagda, the great and good god. And Samain, who had the hostile spirits of the Other-world in his keeping and loosed them once a year at the beginning of winter—what *was* it about the smile on Samain's face that made his head so terrifying . . . ?

Coll tramped on, blind to everything but his inward vision. Supposing he defied those eyeless ones, those keepers of life and death and good and evil? Supposing he did find some way of saving Fand's life—would he have the courage to put it to the test? Was he truly brave enough to accept the cold darkness of endless death for himself in return for life for her?

Of course he was not, he told himself despairingly; yet neither could he accept the fact of Fand's death, and so what other choice had he? And even that was not the end of the problem, for what would become of Fand once he was dead? Who, then, in all these islands, would dare to shelter her from the wrath of the Druids? True, he might manage to survive for a while and escape with her—to the mainland, say. But how would they survive there? How would they endure the terror of that place of mountains and trees dreadfully enclosing them—islanders who had never seen either a forest or a mountain?

Back and forth over the clinging sand of the beach, back and forth in his thoughts—there was no way out, Coll realized dully. And now there was a mist rolling in from the sea, blurring the hard outlines of familiar landmarks, just as his own weariness had begun to blur the sharpness of his thinking. A figure loomed up out of the mist, a figure cloaked and hooded, that came gliding swiftly nearer and nearer until he recognized it as Anu bearing down on him. She peered at him, eyes watchful under painted eyelids, one hand brushing a damp streak of hair back from her face, and her voice was hard as she said,

"I came in search of you, Coll, because I must know. Have you resigned yourself—as the rest of us have?"

"To Fand's death?" Coll asked bitterly. "A strange way for a mother to talk about her daughter!"

"Every sacrifice is somebody's loved one," Anu retorted, and in spite of his weariness, Coll's anger flared up again.

"I am not disputing the need for sacrifice!" he raged. "I am crying out against the slaughter of Fand—you know that! And you know there are hundreds of others Domnall could have chosen instead of her."

"I know nothing of the kind," Anu told him sharply. "All any of us know is that we have angered the gods, and that they demand atonement in the sacrifice we make at this year's Beltane—the best atonement we can offer. And what more can we offer than the blood of a Chief's daughter? We must assume that *this* is Domnall's reasoning, for to think otherwise would be a blasphemy that strikes at all belief in the faith he keeps between us and the gods. And no blasphemer can rule the people of the Boar."

With a despair that almost choked him, then, Coll saw how well Niall had judged the attitude Anu would take. Even if the choice of Fand for sacrifice was an attempt to destroy future opposition to Taran, it was blasphemy to say so. Moreover, for Nectan to try to interfere with that choice would be an act of sacrilege that would certainly cause the people to revolt against him. And Anu had no intention of playing into Domnall's hands by permitting that to happen, for the people needed Nectan now more than they needed Fand in the future.

The decision was there in the face staring at him—the beautiful painted face of the stern mother-goddess protecting her people. The will behind the decision was there in the proud carriage of her tall form. Anu would kill Fand herself rather than let her bring about the disaster Nectan's downfall would spell for the tribe!

Coll spoke his final thought aloud, his gaze never shifting from the eyes staring implacably into his own, yet still felt a sense of shock as Anu admitted the truth of his words. The thought of Clodha flashed into his mind— Clodha, always so ready to spring to Fand's defense, protecting her gentler nature, shielding her even from Niall's good-natured teasing. On impulse he exclaimed,

"Clodha will never consent to this!"

"Clodha will do as I bid," Anu said flatly. "She understands that Domnall must be allowed this present victory if we are to live to fight another day, and she knows she is our hope for the future rule of my line. She will do nothing to endanger that."

"But Taran—" Coll began, "if Domnall succeeds in making him her husband—"

"That," Anu interrupted, "will also be dealt with when the time comes."

A sudden desire to jolt Anu in some way shot through Coll. She was too high-handed in her ways, he thought resentfully, too determined to rule as if they were all children. With sharp sarcasm he asked,

"How will you deal with a marriage accomplished? By showing Clodha how to murder Taran in his sleep?"

"If need be." Anu spoke calmly, but the stern, carved

beauty of her features hardened even further with the words; and shooting a warning glance at Coll from under her painted eyelids, she added,

"And as for Niall, I have already made sure he understands the situation. Niall knows that the people will feel themselves honored by Domnall's choice, and that they will look on any attempt to interfere with it as a sacrilege that could only harm them all. Therefore he accepts that there can be no question of 'saving' Fand. And so it is only you now, Coll, whose foolishness could ruin us."

"Foolishness!" Coll exclaimed, and stared incredulously at her. "You call it foolishness to wish to save your own child from death! Have you *no* feelings, Anu?"

Anu's eyes sparked sudden fire. The beautiful mask of her features cracked to show a face twisted with human emotion, and in a voice that shook she retorted,

"I picked you up off this very beach—bleeding, crippled, and orphaned. I nursed you, cared for you, brought you up—a stranger child—as my own. And you accuse me of having no feelings for the child who *is* my own! By the gods, Coll, be thankful that you are crippled, and will never know how hard it is to have to rule. *Your* heart will break but once—when Fand dies. But how many times do you think I have had to take decisions that broke *my* heart?"

Panting, her eyes blazing now, Anu stared a moment longer at Coll. "And so be warned," she finished. "I will not let all the sorrows I have suffered for my people be in vain. The decision regarding Fand is taken, and nothing will be allowed to interfere with it. Nothing and no one —do you hear, Coll?"

With a sweeping gesture that gathered her cloak

around her she turned and hurried away from him. The mist swallowed up her vanishing figure, and Coll was left alone with a weight of defeat on his heart as cold as the rolling gray waters of the sea before him.

"I warned you," Niall told him as they whispered together in their quarters that night. "Nectan is convinced now that Anu is right, and he has set men to guard Fand wherever she goes. There is nothing we can do to save her."

"And was she right about you also?" Coll asked bitterly. "Was she right about Clodha?"

A sigh from the darkness was his only answer, but stubbornly he persisted, "Because I tell you this, Niall. I have thought of all the consequences to myself, and I am still determined to save Fand. I *must*, do you hear? Reason does not enter into it for me now. I only know that I cannot—I *cannot* accept that she must die. But I am not stupid. I can see the force of Anu's arguments. I will try to think of some plan that will not endanger Nectan's position; and all I ask of you and Clodha now is that you, too, will search your minds for such a plan."

"Do you think all this has suddenly changed us into monsters of unfeeling? Of course we will, you fool!"

Niall's answer came in a voice thick with sudden anger. But it was still assurance that he did not stand completely alone now, Coll thought, and with three minds working on the problem, something would surely occur to one of them. Yet still the weight of the defeat Anu had inflicted was heavy on him, and for long hours he lay awake staring at a vision of the days that might have to be lived through before one of them had even the germ of an idea for saving Fand.

The first of these days dragged itself awake, and brought with it the knowledge of Fand's changed condition. Clodha went everywhere with her, red-eyed as if from secret weeping; and discreetly following came the guard of young men Nectan had appointed. Nectan himself was morose, a surly figure as unapproachable as a wolf nursing a wound. Niall kept a guarded, wooden look on his face, and Anu watched them all with the sharp, careful eyes of a hawk brooding over a threat to its territory.

The ghost of Fand moved silently through the first day, and the second, and the third. Then, on the fourth day from Broichan's visit to the dun, the people of the settlement came with the traditional gift of the tunic she would wear on the day of sacrifice; and with this, they brought a gift of their own devising—a cloak of seal fur.

The tunic was of wool bleached to the purest white, and so finely woven that the whole length of it could have been pulled through the circle of a man's finger ring. The fur of the cloak had been taken from the pelts of very young seals, at the time when the silky brown hair had its richest shine; but Coll was blind to the care that had gone into the making of the gifts, and he watched the pushing, jostling crowd outside the dun with hatred in his heart for their excitement. Then Ibar, the smith's son, shuffled forward, and his hatred melted into pity, for Ibar had dared to bring a small personal gift to Fand, and the unhappiness on his face matched Coll's own.

Fand took the little silver mirror Ibar thrust awkwardly at her. She held it up briefly in front of her, and the grave courtesy of the gesture stilled the murmur of teasing laughter Ibar's move had provoked. The polished silver of the mirror's surface momentarily gave back a reflection as still and ghostly pale as a frost flower, and Coll noticed that only Taran still smiled. But it was the kind of smile, he realized, that owed more to self-congratulation than to amusement at Ibar's love-sick little offering; and even as he clenched his hands on the murderous impulse roused by the smile, he was noting the discovery of one more ally against Taran's plans. Ibar! If only he could think of some way of saving Fand, then surely Ibar would help him with it!

Ogham began haranguing the crowd, his eyes glowing, his high-pitched voice almost incoherent as he raved of the honor that had fallen on them, and once more the excitement mounted until it was near the pitch of hysteria. Coll watched Nectan, dully hoping for some further outburst of the anger he had shown before at Ogham; but for all that Nectan was plainly a man ravaged by grief, he endured in silence, and it was Fand herself who eventually took charge of the situation.

With a gesture that directed all the gifts that had been brought her into Anu's charge, she stepped forward to interrupt Ogham's tirade with a little speech of thanks to the people. Then, with a dignity that yet had something strangely forlorn about it, she turned dismissingly from them; and quietly, glancing back at her with the awed faces of those granted a foretaste of the mystery in the sacrifice to come, they began dispersing back to the settlement.

Fand moved away in the opposite direction, ignoring the hand Nectan stretched out to her, and for a moment

Coll was only one more among those left staring at the small figure making its lonely way toward the ridge behind the dun. Then suddenly he found he was hurrying after her, frantically searching his mind for some words of comfort, yet knowing with despairing certainty that there was no comfort left in all the world now for this forlorn girl.

Fand was heading for the stream that ran down the ridge to water the settlement, and as Coll caught up with her a glance over his shoulder showed him Nectan's guard of young men trailing behind. There would be little or no opportunity to speak privately to her now, he realized, and the words seething in his mind came blurting out,

"I will save you, Fand! I will! *I will!*"

They had reached the stream by this time, and Fand halted there, not looking at him or answering his outburst. The bank at her feet was covered with the primroses that grew freely all over the islands each spring, and casually dropping to one knee, she began picking some of the little yellow flowers. Carefully, as if it mattered, she arranged her bunch, then looking up to meet Coll's eyes at last, she asked gently,

"And even if you did, Coll, what then? Would there be a home for me in all these islands? Could we survive, even if you escaped with me to the mainland?"

Coll felt himself flushing. Fand had thought it all out, he realized, just as he had himself; but being Fand, she was too kind to ask how a cripple could protect anyone —even himself!—against the unknown dangers of the mainland.

"But in any case," Fand spoke again, "you would almost certainly be killed yourself if you tried to save me,

Coll; and it would be stupid for us both to die when one will suffice."

Her fingers began working among the flowers, shredding the petals, and speaking very low she added, "You have never realized it, Coll, but it is some time since I understood your feelings for me. And now, if things had been different—"

She hesitated, her glance going toward the group of young men. They had halted a few yards from herself and Coll, but Niall was with them and he was still approaching.

"If I had not been a cripple, you mean," Coll continued for her. "If I had been able to protect you once we escaped—"

"No," Fand interrupted. "Your lameness has never mattered to me—now or ever. What I meant was—" She hesitated again, the steadiness of her gaze faltering, a flush of pink tingeing her paleness. Then, with an attempt at giving a hard tone to her voice, she finished, "It would only make matters worse for both of us now if I explained my meaning."

Niall was on them before Coll could press for anything further from her, and his face showed that he had guessed the subject of their conversation. He spoke low and quickly, with a backward glance to the group of young men and the air of one making casual conversation.

"I must tell you—I have thought of something. Or at least, Clodha and I have, between us. Your brother, Coll. He has lived all his life with the Druids, after all, and he knows at least some of their magic. We thought it possible—"

"That he could show me some way of saving Fand!"

Coll's heart pounded, his words came in a breathless rush, and Niall muttered warningly,

"Yes—but guard your manner now or these others will suspect us. And remember, it would have to be some way that did not endanger Nectan's position. That was the agreement."

"But if that were possible"—Coll copied Niall's pretense of talking casually—"you and Clodha would support me in it?"

"If it met absolutely with that one provision—yes."

Fand rose to her feet as Niall spoke. Coll reached down a hand to help her, and whispered,

"And if Bran tells me it is possible, will you both accept his assurance? And Fand, will you also believe, and do as I bid?"

Niall nodded agreement to this. Fand did not move or speak, but the sudden hope that shone in her eyes was answer enough, and the thought of the cruelty in disappointing that hope struck Coll like a lance. But at least, he determined, he would not keep her in suspense over it a moment longer than was necessary, and without another word he turned and began hurrying from her.

But he must not run, he warned himself. Not yet—not while he was still in sight of Nectan's guards, or even while he was still in view of the settlement, for that would be sure to rouse suspicions of some kind. With difficulty he kept his haste in bounds, and, as soon as he reckoned it safe to do so, broke into a run.

Bran! The name rang in his mind as he raced toward the private meeting place among the rocks. *Bran!* Why had he not thought of Bran before this? Bran would be able to help him. Bran *must* be able to help him!

He reached the rocks, panting, his lame leg on fire with pain, and stood looking down at the flat rock beside the pool with Fand's game of fidchell still marked out on it and the pebble counters still lying in their squares. He must empty his mind of everything else now, he told himself, and think only of his need for Bran. That was how Bran had said he could be summoned. That was how it must be done.

Coll dropped to his knees beside the fidchell rock. His hands, outstretched before him, clutched two of Fand's pebble counters; his upper body slumped till his cheek rested on the rock's flat surface. Gradually the pressure of his weight hollowed out resting places for his knees in the soft dampness of the sand around it; and gradually all thought except the thought of his need for Bran drained from his mind.

Bran! Bran! Bran . . . !

The name reverberated in a voiceless cry through the empty shell of his mind. There was nothing except the cry—no beach or sea or sky around him, no smell of seaweed or salt water, no sound of seabirds crying, no smoothness of rock against his face or gritty sand hollows gripping his knees. There was no sight, sound, or feeling of any kind, and ultimately there was no time either. The cry existed in a total vacuum. It was. It always had been. It would go on forever, sounding, sounding. . . .

Coll came back to a knowledge of his surroundings at last, feeling completely drained of strength. His body was locked in cramp, and he rolled over, groaning with the pain of returning circulation. There was no sign of Bran; but it would take Bran a long time to reach him, he reminded himself, and settled patiently to wait for that to happen. The day began to fade into late afternoon. The air grew colder. The seabirds wheeling overhead seemed to cry ever more mournfully, and it seemed a dream at first when he looked up to see Bran standing in front of him.

"I came as soon as I heard you calling," Bran said, "but it was a long way from the Ring."

Coll stared up at the slight figure and, wondering how anyone could possibly have "heard" that voiceless cry he had sent out, felt once again the uneasiness that had touched him when Bran had first explained how he could be summoned. But this was no time to indulge such feelings, he reminded himself, and spoke in a firm voice.

"Do you know why I called you?"

Bran knelt down so that their faces were on a level. "At this particular time," he said quietly, "it takes no special powers to know that. Fand is marked for sacrifice, and you love her."

"And so I need your help," Coll told him urgently. "I need you to tell me if there is any way she can be saved from this sacrifice."

Bran gave a hissing intake of breath. A look of misery grew in his eyes, and with a note of desperation in his voice he exclaimed,

"Why could the choice not have fallen on someone who meant nothing to you! I have had so little time, Coll—so little time. . . ."

Coll stared at him in bewilderment. Then he frowned, remembering that Bran had made some similar remark to Fand.

"This is no moment for mysteries, Bran," he said wearily. "Tell me what you mean by that."

Bran gazed full at him, and it seemed to Coll that his thin face grew even thinner, till it was all desolate gray eyes staring at him. He waited, trying hard to hold on to his patience, and Bran said at last,

"There are some things I know, Coll, without understanding how I know them. I cannot help it—it is my nature to be so aware. I knew without having to be told that Fand had been chosen for sacrifice; and I knew that because this was so, my time with you was nearly finished."

Coll hesitated, torn between exasperation and pity. Pity won, and he said gently,

"Bran, I realize I take my life in my hands over this. But my death need not end the time of friendship for you. You would still have Niall, and Clodha, and—if I succeed—Fand herself."

"How blind you are," Bran said. "How very blind, Coll!" He looked away, and added quietly, "But Domnall has told me, of course, that men are always blind to any sorrow not their own."

It was hopeless trying to understand Bran when he talked like this, Coll decided, and with patience fraying still further he pointed out,

"You have still not answered me, Bran. *Is* there any way of saving Fand—some way that will not injure Nectan's position?"

"No way," Bran told him. "No way at all, unless—" The gleaming head turned back to him, the desolate eyes looked full at him again, "—unless Domnall himself rejects her for sacrifice."

"But there could be only one reason for that happening!" Coll exclaimed. "Fand would have to be—" He stopped short, suddenly overcome by anger at the implication in Bran's words, and finished bleakly, "It is not true—what you suggest. And Domnall would guess it was only an attempt to save her. He would never believe such a statement."

"Not if it came from you to start with," Bran agreed. "But if it came from someone else, and if it was put in the form of an accusation against you, *then* he would be forced to take notice of it. And especially so if that accusation came from someone who had no interest in saving Fand; someone whose only concern was to see that the gods received the honor due to them."

"*Ogham!*" The name flashed into Coll's mind. He muttered it aloud, mentally recalling Ogham's rapt, fanatical expression as he harangued the crowd at the ceremony of the gifts, and Bran asked,

"Who did you say?"

"Ogham," Coll told him absently. "The man who finally rescued you after you had been set afloat in the little coracle. He is well known for his devotion to the gods."

Bran's eyes widened in shock, and under his breath he muttered, "*So carefully, then, the gods have planned!*" But Coll was too preoccupied to hear this remark or to notice the change in expression that went with it. There was still a flaw in Bran's suggestion, he was telling himself, and looked up to say,

"But supposing I do manage to trick Ogham into accusing me. Domnall would still have that accusation put to the test. And then he would discover how false it was, and Fand would still die."

Bran rose to his feet and stood looking down at Coll.

"The moment of sacrifice is very carefully timed," he said gravely. "If you can lay your plans so that Domnall has no chance of making such a test until *after* that moment, you will save Fand's life. That, I promise you, for although I do not know how it will happen, I know that it will."

Coll began scrambling up to stand facing him, speaking as he rose. "But you must know how, or you would not be so sure. You must—"

"I tell you I do *not* know! *I do not know!*"

Shouting, Bran interrupted, his eyes blazing, his face suddenly so contorted with anguish that Coll shrank from him. In the silence that fell between them, Bran gradually brought his features under control, and even smiled the ghost of his familiar little smile of self-mockery.

"I have told you before, brother," he said at last. "I have—certain gifts. But they only permit me to see so far, and no farther."

Coll searched the pale face staring into his own. "But you have reasons for speaking as you have done," he ventured; "reasons that go beyond your knowledge of my feelings for Fand."

Bran shook his head. "I speak only as my destiny drives me to speak," he said flatly. "I do only what my destiny drives me to do. Now ask me no more, brother, but remember this. I know Domnall to be a great man, a great scholar, and a great priest. Therefore I know also that he truly believes he does only what the gods command him to do."

"Which will be to kill me!" Vividly, as the words flashed through his mind, Coll pictured the punishment Domnall would inflict on him whether the plan he had in

mind succeeded or failed. But Bran was still talking, asking him,

"Will you keep this in mind—as I will—on Beltane morning?"

Somehow, Coll managed a nod and a mutter of assent to the question. It would be hard for Bran, he realized, to watch the death of the brother he had just come to know; and harder still for him to accept that Domnall, whom he admired so much, would be the one to deal the death-blow.

"Whatever may happen on Beltane morning," he assured Bran, "I shall not blame Domnall for it. You have my promise on that."

The realization that these would probably be his last words to Bran came suddenly to him, and with an attempt at a smile he added,

"Although I shall still wish that our time together could have been longer—brother."

Bran looked at him for a moment in silence, then turned to walk a few steps away. His gaze lifted to where the rays of the setting sun had lit the small clouds in the western sky and transformed them to little floating islands of gold. The cloud islands drifted and broke, like a shining land just glimpsed only to disappear again, and Bran spoke with a note of wistfulness in his voice.

"The land of the Otherworld is in the west."

Coll glanced from the drift of cloud islands to Bran himself. The lifted head was aureoled by the sun's slanting rays. The watching face, outlined against the darkness of the surrounding rocks, was suffused with the same gentle light. Like a dream face hovering pale against the dark of sleep, Coll thought, and stirred uneasily at the mystery his mind had shaped. Yet still his thoughts ran unbidden on—like the face of one of the beautiful, shining dead of the Otherworld itself. . . .

"So they say, anyway." Bran spoke again, still looking westward. "But they say many things about the Otherworld. And who is to know how much is true in these tales, and how much of them men wish to think is true?"

But one thing *was* certain, Coll told himself. There was no share in the Otherworld for one like himself, who would die guilty of sacrilege! He strove hard to stifle the cold terror of this knowledge as Bran turned and came toward him again. They stood face to face, and he was touched to see something of the same forlorn dignity in Bran as he had seen earlier in Fand. Impulsively he reached out to clasp the other's shoulder, and Bran said,

"One thing more I have been permitted to see now. Whatever you may think at this moment, we two *shall* meet again in the Otherworld. And so—for a time at least—good-bye, brother."

One hand came up to lie gently over Coll's hand for a moment; then he was gone, moving lightly and quickly as always. Coll watched until the last flutter of the sandy-red cloak had been swallowed up by the darkening day, then moved off toward the dun, with his mind busily revolving around the scheme of drawing Ogham into his plan for saving Fand.

9
Sacrifice

All through the night the people of the islands had been on the move, for the festival to celebrate the coming of the summer god, Belenos, began with the moonrise before Beltane morning.

By the dusk of that night, the people of Nectan's settlement had all their cattle herded and ready to drive before them to the Ring, where the Druids would invoke the fertility magic of Belenos to bless them as they passed between the great Beltane bonfires. The three precious balks of timber for creating the sacred spark of Beltane fire had already been transported to the Ring, where they would stand in the shape of two uprights and a crosspiece. And from all those competing for the honor, nine young men had been chosen to join with those from other settlements in the magic number of the nine times nine men who would twirl the crosspiece in its sockets, and so create the friction to produce the spark.

By dusk, also, the banks of the stream were crowded

with people bathing. Ornaments gleamed on freshly oiled skin; and among men as well as women, the vanity of the Celt showed itself in a great activity of combing hair and bleaching it to the straw-gold color that was their hallmark of beauty.

Inside Nectan's dun there was a haze of smoke from the hearth where the fire had been stamped out and its ashes cleared in preparation for the new fire that would be lit from embers of the magic Beltane flames. Coll's eyes met those of Ogham through this haze, and quickly he looked away from the question in their glance. The seed he had dropped into that strange mind had taken root, he realized, but he must not encourage it to flower as yet, or the timing that was so important to his plan would be ruined.

He looked at Nectan, and all the anger he had felt against him turned to pity, for it was clear that Nectan was now reaching his breaking point. His hands were shaking as he fastened the great gold buckle of the belt around his tunic; and his face was so ravaged by grief now that even Anu's skillful use of the *ruam* she used to paint her own cheeks could not disguise the traces of his mourning for Fand.

Anu came into the dun, and Nectan spoke in a rapid undertone to her. She answered in the same low voice, and Coll caught nothing of the words except "—too late for that now—too late . . ." Then Anu turned to announce to them all,

"She is ready."

Outside the dun was a world of moonlight peopled by pale, waiting faces and a dark blur of cattle restlessly moving. The light frost that so often brought in the month of May nipped the air. Six bearers stood shoulder-ing a litter that had Fand huddled down in it. The white bull on which she would ride into the Ring stood to one side of the litter with the boy, Ibar, holding its headrope. Coll moved to Ibar's side and whispered,

"Remember to keep the hood of your cloak up, and no one will suspect."

"You can count on me."

Ibar's whispered reply came with all the eagerness he had shown ever since Coll had begged his help in the plan; but with only a casual nod to show he had heard it, Coll turned to watch Nectan and Anu and Clodha taking their places behind the litter.

Nectan's voice rang out in the signal for the procession to start, and Ibar jerked the bull's headrope, pulling it forward with him. The creature bellowed a loud and mournful protest, and to the sound of an answering dis-cord of protest from the waiting cattle, Ibar walked it forward to lead the litter bearers. Coll moved to join the other members of Nectan's household falling in behind him and Anu, and walked along with his eyes following the small dark figure swaying on the shoulders of the litter bearers.

Fand had not looked around once, he noticed; not even when Nectan and Anu appeared. And wondered what she was thinking now, huddled down with that cloak of rich seal fur over her white robe of sacrifice. . . . Did she still trust him? She was aware of the strangeness in Bran, much more aware than Niall and Clodha; and so it had been easier to persuade her his plan would work than it had been to persuade the other two. But all that had happened two nights ago, and there had been time enough since then for doubts to gather in her mind; time enough for her to slip back despairing into her cold shadow world....

The procession had moved slowly up the sloping ground of the north-by-east arc that formed the first part of the path to the Ring. Now that climb was behind them and they were swinging around to head northwest over open moor, but their pace was still the slow, deliberate pace of the bull in front of the litter.

From the heart of the procession came a burst of pipe music—wild, sweet notes that went scattering eerily over the desolate, moonlit stretches of the moor; and from somewhere far in the distance, where the people of other settlements were converging on the Ring, came the sound of a ghostly answering strain. Nectan's harper, Emban, unslung his harp to finger it softly as he walked, and voices took up the song he played, spreading it farther and farther back through the ranks of the procession.

Was Taran also singing as he walked? Coll asked himself the question with a sense of outrage flaming in his mind, then smiled grimly at the thought of the surprise in store for Taran. His gaze roamed over the moor and picked out the dark shape of another settlement's procession moving to join their own. Gartnait's people, he thought, automatically noting the direction from which they came. He became aware that Niall had eased forward to walk alongside him, and after a while Niall whispered,

"Have you spoken to Ogham again?"

"Not yet. I have to give him the impression now that I do not want to talk further." Coll answered low, alert for a turn of the head from Anu walking directly in front of him. "And then I must make it seem he is forcing answers out of me."

Niall grunted a doubtful acceptance of this, then dropped gradually back to his former position. The sound of voices mingling with harp and pipe music grew louder. The grumbling, bellowing cattle kept up a discordant undertone, and Coll wondered what the people of the Raven and the Deer were making of the din, for this was not the way *they* arrived at the festival of Beltane.

They came silently to the Ring, moving furtively over the moor in little, secret groups. *They* stood huddled on the fringes of the crowd inside the Ring, raising no shout of joy as the blood ran from the sacrifice. . . .

Coll caught himself up in his thoughts, aware suddenly of the way he had been emphasizing the word "they" in his mind. As if the people of the Deer and the Raven were somehow less or more than human, he told himself —like the witches and fairies and other curious creatures of storytelling time in the dun. And to think like that, as wise old Conamaill had often warned, was a mistake that gave these tribes an advantage of terror over the people of the Boar. He must dismiss such thoughts from his mind, and concentrate rather on what he still had to say to Ogham!

Head down, Coll plodded along, reviewing the conversation he had had with Ogham as they walked the round of the guard posts together the previous night. He had said enough then, he decided, to rouse suspicion against himself; yet not enough to make Ogham go rushing to Nectan with his suspicions. He had also taken care to let Ogham see how well he could control the guard dogs; and, he hoped, that was something else which would feed Ogham's suspicions to the point where he would feel obliged to pursue them. So far, then, everything had gone exactly as he had planned. But once he did allow Ogham to trap him into further conversation, he would simply have to rely on his wits to find words that would turn suspicion into certainty.

The distance to the Ring slid slowly past, and as processions from one settlement after another converged upon it, the path followed by those of Nectan's settlement became a wide, crawling river of cattle and humans, all moving at the slow pace of the white bull stepping in the lead. The sky darkened into the hour before dawn; then, as it began gradually to lighten again, the shapes of the four Guard Stones rose tall against it. The single pillar of the Gatekeeper rose even taller beyond these four; and from either side of the Gatekeeper there was a sullen gleam from the two arms of loch water enclosing the site of the Ring.

The procession flowed slowly past the Guard Stones. The white bull reached the Gatekeeper, and now it was the stones of the Ring itself that rose into view. Coll felt the old, familiar shiver of awe that this first sight of them always bred in him, and knew from the spreading hush that those behind him were being similarly affected.

The ranks of the procession narrowed as it crossed the thin strip of land that ran between the two lochs and formed a Y shape with them. From the jostling of this shift in the order of march, a hand came out to grab Coll's arm, and he heard the sound he had been waiting for—Ogham's voice whispering urgently,

"I must talk with you again."

"No!" Coll made to pull away, as if guiltily surprised. "There is no more to talk about. Why should there be?"

"Because you have already said too much—or was it too little? Do you hear?" Ogham's hand pressed harder on Coll's arm. "That set me thinking. *And my thoughts frighten me this Beltane morning!*"

Ogham's voice fairly hissed on the last words, and in tones that were rough with pretended fear, Coll shot back at him,

"Be quiet, will you! Do you think *I* am not frightened?"

"But you have nothing to fear—not if it was the truth you spoke to me last night!" The hand on Coll's arm pressed tighter yet. "If you *were* only talking in general terms—as you claimed you were—and not of some particular case."

Coll jerked hard against the restraining clutch. "I have had enough of this—let me go!"

"Not till you answer me," Ogham whispered fiercely. "*Were* you talking in a general sense? *Or did you have Fand and yourself in mind?*"

"Oh, gods!" Coll's voice came out in a gasp. "Do you want me killed, Ogham? Of course I was not thinking of myself and Fand. How could I be? And what about the dogs, roaming loose at night? *They* would have made it impossible!"

"Not for a godless young man bent on his own selfish purpose," Ogham retorted. "Especially for one who knows how to handle the dogs as you do."

"Your head is turned with thoughts of the gods!" Fiercely Coll jerked his arm away and glared at Ogham. "But I will not listen to any more of such dangerous talk."

"It frightens you, eh?" Ogham pounced on his words, and worried them. "But you were already frightened before I spoke. You said so, a moment ago. Why, Coll? What have you done that frightens you? Are you afraid I have guessed correctly about you and Fand?"

Coll glanced swiftly around and saw the procession behind them breaking up into a rush of figures heading for the northwestern aspect of the Ring—the only aspect from which the people were permitted to enter.

"Tell me the truth, Coll." Ogham's voice came again, and he glanced back to the thin, fanatical face beside him. There was enough of the grayish daylight now to reveal its features, and with a little shock of pity he saw the nervous twitching that affected them and the distress in the burning brightness of the eyes. Ogham really was touched with some holy madness, he realized, then roughly dismissed pity with the thought of the sacrificial knife descending on Fand.

"Go home, Ogham," he said cruelly. "The truth is that you are touched in your mind. Go home before you have everyone laughing at your mad guesses. And, old man though you are, remember how close I am to Nectan before you insult me so again!"

Swinging on his heel with the last word, Coll ran to join the scattered, scurrying mass of figures heading for the northwest aspect of the Ring, calculations tumbling hurriedly through his mind as he ran.

He would have to lose himself in that mass now, for now Ogham really was convinced. He had taken the bait so carefully laid—swallowed it whole! And those last, deliberate taunts would add a fine edge of anger to his convictions. He would go straight to Nectan now, Coll warned himself, and demand action on what he *thought* he had discovered. But Nectan would not be so easily convinced. It would not take him long to disprove the accusation in Ogham's story, and then the whole timing of the plan would misfire!

Coll's thoughts raced on, faster than his limping steps could carry him. He would have to be very careful to keep out of Nectan's reach for a while—long enough at least to make sure Nectan had no chance of arriving at the truth behind the argument with Ogham. And fanatic as he was, that would be the very thing to goad Ogham himself into even more drastic action!

The causeway that spanned the wide ditch circling the outside of the Ring was crowded with people pressing forward to pass between the two tall stones flanking the permitted point of entry. Determinedly Coll forced himself into this press of bodies, and was carried with it over the causeway. The wide stretch of moor enclosed by the sixty great stones of the Ring opened out before him; and breaking free to the outskirts of those buffeting their way still farther into this central area, he halted to recover his breath. With his back pressed to one of the enclosing stones, then, he surveyed the scene of the Beltane sacrifice.

There was an upward slope to the ground ahead of him, a slope running from the northwest to the southeastern aspect of the Ring; but toward this southeastern aspect—the one from which the Druids would enter—the slope leveled out to form a plateau.

At the near edge of the plateau, and thus observable from every point of the slope leading up to it, stood a low altar of turf with a bare, earthen surface. The altar was heaped around on every side except that to the southeast, with straw and dry peat; and wryly, before his gaze moved on, Coll noted these preparations for the burning of Fand's body.

The fire machine was also ready. It stood outside the Ring, on a high, flat-topped mound rising just beyond the causeway over the ditch at the southeast entrance. Its two wooden uprights, with the wooden crosspiece socketed into them, loomed tall and dark against the gray wash of light in the sky. The rope that had been wound around the crosspiece had its two ends dangling free. And still as a frieze of dark statues against the gray sky, the nine times nine men chosen to create the Beltane fire stood ready for their turn to pull on the rope, and so set the crosspiece whirling and building up friction for the sacred spark.

Everything, Coll thought, seemed the same as it always had in the dawn hour before a Beltane sunrise—the altar, the fire machine, the stones of the Ring towering hugely around, the dark slope clotted with even darker groups of milling people, the susurration of whispering voices and feet swishing through the heathery grass of the moor. But it was still not quite the same—not for him, anyway; for he had not come like those whispering others to share in the worship of the gods. He had come to profane that worship.

Terror ran suddenly in his blood at the thought—the cold terror of a condemned man realizing he has just surveyed the scene of his own execution; and beside that terror, his next fear seemed a trivial one.

He was surrounded now, he realized, by the small figures of the Raven and the Deer people, standing in their usual places far back on the outskirts of the people of his own tribe. He could see the shape of the conical feathered caps the men wore sprouting dimly from the heads nodding around him. He could hear voices muttering in the guttural speech of the old tongue. And even in this gray light they had seen he was not one of their own kind, for the heads were nodding at him and the muttering had a hostile tone to it.

Quickly Coll reached up to pull the hood of his cloak forward over his face. It was time for his next move in any case, he excused the nervous haste of the gesture, for now he could see the white bull entering the Ring with Ibar still at its head. And Fand, transferred from her litter, was seated on the creature's back.

With a sudden thrust and a movement forward, he broke clear of the hostile group around him. Then rapidly he worked his way through the crowded mass of his own people until he was within touching distance of Ibar. The boy had remembered to keep the hood of his cloak up. Coll drew a breath of relief as he saw this, for everything now hung on the fact that—in this dim light at least—there was nothing to distinguish his own appearance from that of Ibar's cloaked and hooded figure.

Head down, Coll strove to keep his position in the mob surging forward with the advancing bull; and from the corner of his eye saw Ibar stumble, as if knocked off balance by the press of bodies around him. The stumble became a fall, and instantly, Coll was at the heart of the confused swirl of movement around the sprawled form.

Ibar staggered up at his side. The leading rope passed unsuspected from the hand of one cloaked and hooded figure to that of the other; and as the confusion resolved, it was Coll who plodded on leading the bull while Ibar was swallowed up by the crowd.

The first of the teams of nine men had begun working to produce the spark for the Beltane fires. Coll heard the whir of the crosspiece in its sockets as he led the bull slowly on, but did not dare to look up to confirm this. Nor did he even dare to risk showing his face with a sideways glance at Fand until he had finally reached the west side of the altar, and pulled the beast to a halt there.

Cautiously then, he inched his head round toward her and saw how she sat huddled, her head bent, her face hidden by the forward sweep of her long hair. Her sealskin cloak was spread out over the bull's back now, so that she was dressed only in the long white tunic the women had woven for her death robe. Coll's swiftly traveling look came down to her hands, gripping hard on the part of the cloak that lay across the bull's neck, and pity for the terror in the gesture overwhelmed him.

He risked a quick glance around in search of Ogham, and saw him standing with Nectan and Anu, immediately in front of the altar. All three, he realized, were deep in some fierce, low-toned argument, their heads together, their hands furiously gesticulating. Every now and then, one of them would glance furtively around as if afraid of being overheard; and with a thrill of triumph, Coll saw how Nectan shook his head at Ogham and began to turn away from the argument.

His glance came back to Fand. Her face was still hidden, her head despairingly bent, her hands grasping hard on the seal fur. The exchange with Ibar had happened so quickly and in such confusion, Coll realized, that perhaps she was still not aware of it. He whispered her name. There was a momentary relaxing of the tightly clenched hands, and he whispered again,

"Courage, Fand. Ogham has taken the bait!"

Now Fand did look up, staring straight ahead to where the pale gray wash of the sky was becoming very faintly tinged with pink. The flush of color spread slowly from behind the rising ground to the east of the Ring; and like a herald announcing that first pale flag of dawn, a strain of harp music came also from east of the Ring.

Silence gripped the huge crowd gathered there; and as the harp music grew louder, the only other sounds to be heard were the steady whir from the rotating crosspiece of the fire machine, and the restless bellowing of the cattle herded outside the Ring.

The harp music drew still nearer, and now there were voices raised in tune to it; first, the sweet high notes of Abiris, the poet, then a deep melodious chorus of men's voices responding to his hymn in praise of the summer god, Belenos. Coll felt a fresh prickle of terror at the sacrilege he was about to commit against the god, but a quick glance at Fand steadied his nerve again. He stared at the southeast entrance to the Ring, counting the moments that must pass before he could throw back his hood and let the unexpected sight of his presence provide the final goad to Ogham's fevered imagination.

Louder, nearer . . . The voices were almost at the Ring. The flush in the sky was deepening. The soaring voice of Abiris reached a peak of exaltation, and suddenly there was a column of Druids walking three abreast across the causeway and into the Ring, the white of their robes palely gleaming, the crimson of their cloaks blocked darkly over the white.

They passed from within the shadow of the stones that momentarily dwarfed them with contrasting height; and, still in a column of three, moved slowly forward, one

order of the College of Druids to each column. Abiris led
the order of poets. Broichan led the order of seers. And
walking between these two, Domnall led the order of
priests.

The threefold column circled sunwise from its point of
entrance to the Ring, voices still melodiously rising in
time to the slow-stepping pace. The white-and-crimson
forms halted, their three columns merging to form a single arc behind the altar, while Abiris, Domnall, and
Broichan came forward to it. And from the place where
he had walked at the tail of the procession, Bran came
forward also.

The three Druids ranged themselves behind the altar,
with Domnall between the other two. Abiris struck the
final chord of the music from his harp, and as the singing
soared to the crescendo that marked its end, Bran moved
forward to kneel with outstretched hands in front of
Domnall.

A knife lay on his spread palms—a long, thin-bladed
knife that shone dimly in the dim half-light of dawn.
Bran raised the knife high, and in the moment that he did
so, Coll threw back the hood from his face. Turning, he
stared straight at the group made by Nectan, Anu, and
Ogham; and immediately, as if there had been some
magnetic pull in his stare, Ogham's head swiveled toward
him. The thin features stiffened and stayed fixed in an
expression of surprise; then, swinging back to Nectan,
Ogham snatched at the other's arm and pointed.

Nectan turned toward Coll, his face echoing the moment of surprise on Ogham's face, and Anu turned with
him. Then Nectan's eyes dropped away, and he made a
quick, fierce gesture that stilled the urgent words Ogham

was forcing on him. Coll looked toward the altar again and saw Domnall standing erect, the knife he had accepted from Bran held with two hands in front of his face. Bran stood by his side, slight and small in his white tunic beside Domnall's bulk, his face turned toward the silent, watching crowd.

This was the moment! Coll reached up to Fand, gripped his hands around her waist, and helped her to slide to the ground beside him. She was trembling, and the hand she rested on his arm was icy. Her feet touched the ground, and he whispered,

"Have courage still! If Ogham fails us, *I* will speak!"

Taking one of the ice-cold hands in his, then, he drew her gently on a step; and as they moved, Ogham threw off the restraining grip Nectan had laid on him. Plunging forward to the altar, he shouted in a voice that cracked with urgency,

"Hold, Domnall! You profane the gods with this sacrifice!"

Fand shrank away behind Coll. Domnall lowered the knife from the ritual position before his face, and stared in astonished outrage at the figure now struggling to prevent Nectan from renewing his grip. With the knife pointing in accusation, Domnall snapped at Nectan,

"Is this man mad?"

Ogham's shout cut across Nectan's attempt to answer. "I am not mad, but I have knowledge denied to you, and it is this. Fand is no longer fit for sacrifice, *for she is no longer a virgin!*"

"He is talking nonsense!" Fiercely Nectan's voice followed on Ogham's outburst. "I have guarded my daughter as I would my own life, and she *is* still virgin. I swear to that!"

"You swear to what you do not know. Ask *him*!" With a shaking hand pointed at Coll, Ogham loosed a torrent of accusation.

"*He* spoke to me last night, asking whether it had ever happened that a man had taken the maiden marked for sacrifice, and whether such a man could escape the vengeance of the gods. And it moved in my mind that he might have been talking about himself and Fand, for he had a guilty look as he spoke, and it is well known he would have married Fand if that had been permitted. And so this morning I asked him outright if he had been talking about his own case, and he gave me answers that told me I had guessed the truth."

"Domnall!" Anu stepped forward, her voice and figure commanding attention. "This man's mind is unhinged by devotion to the gods. That also is well known. And my daughter is virgin. That I know, as only a mother can, for I see to it that she keeps strictly to her quarters at night with the other maidens and is guarded there by the dogs that roam free from sunset to sunrise around our dun."

Domnall turned to cast a brief, anxious glance at the ever-deepening color in the sky, and Ogham shouted at Anu,

"But do you know how Coll can gentle those dogs? Do you know how easily and safely he can step from his own quarters to those of Fand because of that?"

"Come here!" Domnall swung round from his survey of the sunrise signs to command Coll, then glared at Ogham, Nectan, and Anu. "And you others, keep silence while I question him."

It was full daylight now, and Coll could see clearly the fierce anger that distorted Domnall's features. There was outrage on the faces of Broichan and Abiris also, but Bran's expression had not changed. His gaze, as he stood at Domnall's side, was fixed unblinkingly on space. The pale face turned toward the watching crowd had an almost inhuman composure.

Coll moved forward, his mind racing ahead of his reluctant feet. Domnall must strike the knife into Fand at the moment the first ray of sunrise touched the altar. The whole magic of the sacrifice depended on that timing, for this was the moment that revealed the power of the gods, and it was the blood of the sacrifice that united the people with them. But Domnall could not strike so long as there was any doubt in his mind over Fand. He could not risk profaning the gods with such an action. . . .

Time! Coll snatched at the one clear guideline in the feverish race of his thoughts. He must play for time. The doubt must be kept alive in Domnall's mind—at least until the moment of sunrise was past. And after that . . . ?

Coll's mind spun in total confusion as he tried to force his thoughts past this point. He halted in front of Domnall, and cast one more look, a long look of pleading, at Bran; but if Bran had any more knowledge than he had already revealed he was still giving no sign of it. The pale face was still expressionless, the brilliant gray eyes still blankly staring at nothing.

"Look at me!" Domnall's voice sounded harshly, startling Coll's attention away from Bran. "Fix your eyes on mine and answer the charge against you."

Coll met the eyes frowning down on him, and immediately felt his resolution weakening. There was some strange power in those eyes. They were boring into his own and he could not look away from them. They were drawing an answer out of him, forcing him to speak, and to speak truly.

Time . . . a small warning voice repeated in his bemused mind, *play for time. . . .*

"I—" Croakingly he formed his first word, his mind desperately scurrying away from the power probing it, despairingly seeking the evasive form of answer he needed.

A shout from the mound outside the Ring broke the stretched silence between himself and Domnall, a shout of triumph from the fire makers whirling the crosspiece. Domnall jerked toward the sound, and with the contact between them broken, Coll's eyes flashed to follow his gaze.

The whirling ends of the crosspiece had at last struck sparks onto the linen stuffed into the sockets of the uprights, and the linen was blazing raggedly. The Beltane fire had been made, and already eager hands were stretching out with torches to catch flame from it. Coll's eyes shifted from the mound to the glow that heralded the sun's first appearance over the horizon. It needed only a few more moments' delay, he realized, and the whole ritual of sacrifice would be ruined. . . .

The realization brought the words he had sought leaping into his mind; and with a thrill of triumph he recognized the double meaning that could be read into them, and how that would deceive Domnall.

"Answer me!" Domnall swung back to him, glaring as he rasped out the order; and reluctantly, like a man forced at last to confession, Coll obeyed.

"I—I have spoiled the sacrifice."

Domnall's face contorted in a fresh access of rage. The

hand holding the bronze knife flew high, and as he poised it momentarily to drive it down into Coll's heart, Bran cried out in sudden protest. The first ray of the rising sun transformed the poised blade to a ray of glittering gold, and Domnall struck with it. But in the flash of time it took for the blade to descend, Bran threw himself in front of Coll, and the blade buried itself deep in his back.

With a gasping cry, Bran jerked under the impact. The hands clutching at Coll flew wide. He staggered, and straightened again, with blood pumping out to crimson the white of his tunic. For a moment that seemed never-ending he stood motionless, a slight figure of crimson and white, the rays of the sun edging over the horizon making a golden crown of his hair and glittering on the haft of the knife transfixing him.

Then he fell, his body dropping face-down over the altar that was suffused with a sudden gold of sunlight in the moment of his falling. The blood running from his tunic spread in a bright stain over the bare brown earth of the altar's surface; and like a wild wind rising, the keening voice of Broichan cried,

"The prophecy! See how the prophecy is fulfilled!"

A long sighing moan rose from the watching crowd, and as it faded, the body on the altar quivered and stretched. Then abruptly the crimson pumping of blood ceased, and Bran was dead.

For a long moment after that, no one moved; no one spoke or shifted his gaze from the slight figure stretched out on the sunlit altar. Druids and common people alike remained as if frozen into the attitudes that had witnessed Bran's death. Then Domnall stepped forward, and with tears trickling down the deep furrows of his face, spoke quietly into the stupefied silence.

"Here is now a mystery performed before us, for Bran is dead instead of the sacrifice that was intended. He is dead in a manner that observes all the terms of the prophecy concerning him—because of you and your actions, and in a manner and time of his own choosing."

The quiet tones faltered, then picked up firmly again. "I mourn for Bran, whom I taught and cherished. But I rejoice in his death, for he was young and beautiful, and without blame; a perfect sacrifice for your atonement. Rejoice with me, therefore, in the death of Bran...."

Abiris struck his harp in the first chord of the Beltane hymn, and a harmony of harps echoed it from all the other members of the poets' order. The first words of praise to Belenos, the sun god of summer, rose in a massed chorus of voices, and from the mound outside the Ring a procession of nine times nine torchbearers advanced to set the altar ablaze with the sacred fires of Beltane.

Coll came out of the daze that held him to see Domnall turning to beckon to two of his fellow Druids. He whispered to them, and all three advanced to halt in front of Coll and Fand.

"Go to your parents!" Abruptly Domnall addressed Fand; and backing white-faced from him, she fled to the shelter of Nectan's arms. Domnall turned grimly on Coll.

"Bran's death does not absolve you from guilt," he said. "And presently you will discover what that means for both you *and* the girl."

10
Trial

Coll shifted uncomfortably in the bonds the Druids had used to tie him to one of the Guard Stones. He had been there for over an hour now, listening to the sounds of celebration from the Ring, but it was not the cramping feel of the ropes that troubled him, nor even the threat that Domnall had made against Fand.

Fand would be safe enough, he assured himself, for Anu could use all the special skills of women to prove she was still a virgin; and that would clear her of Ogham's charge. As for being tied like this, that was a minor and passing discomfort compared to the torment of his thoughts about Bran!

Had Bran intended from the very start to throw himself in front of that knife?

Once again Coll heard the echo of the question that, above everything else, obsessed him now. The vision of the bright blade descending flashed once more before his eyes, and carefully he tried to reconstruct his final conversation with Bran.

They had been talking at cross-purposes then, he realized, with himself thinking that *he* would be the one to die, and Bran knowing otherwise. *"I have not had time —not nearly enough time. . . ."* Now he understood what Bran had meant by that! *Now*, now that Bran was dead, he understood the bitterness of regret, the longing for life behind that doomed cry!

But for all that, Coll realized, Bran had still not known the exact moment of his death or what the manner of it would be; for he had said himself that his gifts permitted him to see only so far into the future. And so it stood to reason that he had leaped forward on impulse, with only a sudden desperate resolve at rescue in his mind. He *must* have acted on impulse, for surely no boy of fourteen would willingly leap toward such a death!

And yet . . . Supposing in the very moment of his leap Bran had realized that this *was* to be the manner of his death? Supposing he had known, in that last terrible moment as the blood pumped from him, how strangely he had fulfilled the prophecy about himself? Would he have been resigned to that knowledge as he died?

Memory touched Coll's mind again, the memory of the little smile Bran had so often worn; and suddenly he knew the reason for the self-mockery in it. It had simply been an indication of the way Bran had learned to live with his destiny, he realized. It was his way of belittling it—of making it seem less tragically important to himself. And perhaps—perhaps he had even worn that little smile as he died. . . .

Coll hoped so. He let his head sink forward, wearily hoping that it had indeed been so. Yet still the hope could not rid his mind's eye of the slight figure standing transfixed and bloodstained in the first glory of sunrise; and groaning inwardly, he looked up again.

The smoke from the Beltane fires was billowing high now, and in the confused murmur of sound coming from the Ring he could distinguish the bellowing of the cattle that were being driven round and around the flames, and the high, chanting voices of the Druids pronouncing the words of blessing on them. He could see movement too now, on the path from the Ring, the movement of a group of figures coming toward him.

The figures drew nearer and he recognized Domnall, with Abiris and Broichan on either side of him; and, following behind these three, Nectan and the whole Council of Elders, with Nectan's womenfolk in their midst.

Coll's heart raced as he made out Fand walking between Anu and Clodha. She was wearing her sealskin cloak again, he saw, one nervous hand clutching the shining brown fur to her throat, her head craning anxiously forward in search of him as the close-ranked party of Councillors swept her forward to the Guard Stones.

The Druids reached the stone to which he was tied, and moved on to halt in a little group some yards to his left. Nectan and his party halted in front of him, but considerably farther away than the Druids' position. They were to be mere spectators at his trial, Coll realized, except possibly for those Domnall might wish to call as witnesses. His gaze came back to Domnall, now moving to stand slightly in front of the other two Druids; and as the frowning glance met his own, the rapid pounding of his heart steadied unaccountably to its usual beat.

"Coll, son of Roth, you are now on trial for your life."

Domnall's harsh voice broke the waiting stillness. "The charge is sacrilege, on two counts. First, that you did despoil a virgin named for sacrifice to the gods; and second, that you did attempt by this means to prevent that sacrifice from being made. Speak to these charges, therefore; and we three, being the number of Druids the law requires to hear your answers, will pass judgment on them."

"The first charge is false." His voice firm, eyes steadily meeting Domnall's gaze, Coll defended himself. Then glancing toward Anu, he added, "Let Anu speak, and she will prove that."

The three Druids turned toward Anu, and Domnall beckoned her to come toward him. She hesitated, glancing uncertainly at Fand and then at Nectan before moving in response to the beckoning hand. Domnall nodded to indicate that she should speak, and with her features hardening to their usual stern composure she told him,

"I do not know the meaning of my foster son's actions today, nor had Nectan any foreknowledge of them. But this I can say now in his defense. At your command, and also following my own desire, I have had my daughter Fand questioned and examined by a panel of married women who were instructed to determine whether or not she is still virgin. These women were sworn on pain of death to be truthful in their report, which I now witness, and which is that Fand is still undoubtedly a virgin woman."

Domnall's frown deepened, and his glance turned to Ogham, peering white-faced and tense from among the rest of the Councillors.

"Then how do you account for this man's accusation?" he asked. "He said that your foster son had as good as confessed to stealing out at night from his own quarters to those of the girl."

"I can speak to that," Niall announced suddenly.

"And I!" Clodha chimed in, and with a glance at one another, each moved a pace forward.

"Coll shares his quarters with me," Niall said, "and I swear on my life he has made no such night expedition as Ogham claims."

"And Fand shares her quarters with me," Clodha added. "I would have known if she had received a man into her bed, but this she has never done."

Domnall turned toward Coll. "So," he said, "it appears there is no guilt attaching to the girl. And since she is innocent, the evidence also clears you of the first count in the charge—"

"But not of the second count!"

Ogham broke forward, shouting, to interrupt Domnall, and glared at Coll, his face working with anger. "You used me!" he accused. "You planted thoughts and ideas in my mind that led me to believe you had committed this sacrilege, knowing full well I would not permit the gods to be affronted with a spoiled sacrifice. And you timed the planting of these ideas so that I would be forced to interrupt the ceremony with my accusation— knowing full well again that Domnall would see it simply as an attempt to save the girl if you had accused yourself of the crime! Is that not so?"

Thrusting his face to within inches of Coll's, he repeated passionately, "Is that not so? You *did* use me to try to prevent Fand being sacrificed? And that makes you guilty—guilty—*guilty* on the second count!"

"Remove this man!"

Domnall's voice thundered out as Coll hastily rolled his head aside from the livid, shouting face thrust into his own, and for a moment there was a noisy scuffling around him as Nectan and some of the Councillors pulled Ogham away. Domnall's voice rose powerfully over the hubbub.

"The second count of the charge still stands—that this man did try to prevent the sacrifice appointed to be made. Let him now speak to the second count."

The scuffling figures were suddenly still, and all eyes turned to Coll. His gaze moved quickly over the faces so intently watching him, and rested on that of Fand. It was finished, he thought tiredly. She was safe at last, and so what was the point of fighting for his own life? Anything he could say, after all, would only betray the secret of the friendship between himself and Bran; and that would be a needless cruelty to Bran's memory for it would make him less than perfect in Domnall's eyes.

His gaze shifted from Fand back to the stern, lined face confronting him, and Domnall said quietly,

"You were of one blood, you and Bran. Did he ever speak to you? Did you know what he meant to do today? Did you plan between you to prevent the sacrifice of the girl?"

It had been strange, Coll thought, to see the tears Domnall had shed for Bran—strange to think that stern old man had any of the juice of human feeling in him! Yet Bran had known it was there. Bran had admired Domnall, and perhaps loved him too. A lie—one kindly lie was all that was needed to keep him forever as he had always been for Domnall—*"young and beautiful, and without blame."* Shrugging, he answered,

"Nectan taught me as you instructed—a Druid has no

kin. Therefore I have never spoken to Bran, nor he to me, and everything I did sprang from my own mind."

"Then why should Bran have thrown himself into the path of the knife to save you?" Domnall demanded.

"How can I tell you that?" Coll countered wearily. "It came as great a surprise to me as it did to you, for all I had in my mind was the trick I had played on Ogham in order to delay the sacrifice of the girl, and so possibly save her."

"You hear him? You hear his confession?" Domnall swung around to call out to the group of listening faces, and turning toward them also, Broichan intoned,

"Hear the punishment for sacrilege. Hear the doom of this man! That he be tied to the Gatekeeper at the sun's setting this day, and shot to the death with the golden arrows of the death god, Samain, from the bows of the Druids there assembled. And his body, departing from this earthly life, shall become a creature cursed and mourning that wanders alone in darkness forever."

There was a sudden stir in the ranks of the Councillors, then Nectan called loudly,

"If Coll is killed my people's only hope of safety from the raiders dies with him. Hear me on this, Domnall!"

Domnall drew himself up to his full height. "Your foster son has confessed to sacrilege," he exclaimed indignantly. "Do you dispute the punishment for that crime?"

"No—but I dispute the guilt you have found in him!" Nectan came thrusting forward, his jaw set aggressively. "I say that his confession was only one of intent to commit sacrilege, and that the gods saved him from this crime by providing Bran for sacrifice!"

"He cast doubt upon the fitness of your daughter for sacrifice," Domnall retorted. "That, in itself, was a sacrilege."

"But does it not strike you as strange," Nectan argued, "that *he* should be the one to cast this doubt—he, who is Bran's brother? You wondered why Bran should have thrown himself in front of the knife, Domnall—forgetting the blood ties that you denied to both these young people. But what if the natural strength of this blood tie was the very thing the gods had counted on to ensure their purpose with Bran? Would not this make Coll only a tool of their will? And so how *can* he be judged guilty now of any crime?"

Abiris the poet said suddenly, "It seems stranger still that Ogham, whom the gods chose to lift Bran from the very arms of Lir—Ogham, who brought him finally ashore to face his destiny—should also be the unknowing instrument of that destiny."

Abiris was a quiet man, dreamy-eyed almost to the point of seeming vacant, and his seldom-raised voice now had an effect that Nectan had not been able to achieve. A stillness fell, a stillness that seemed full of the eerie suggestion in his words.

"What is this hope of safety that will die with Coll?" The clear, precise voice of Gartnait came matter-of-factly into the charged atmosphere. "We have a right to hear that, Domnall."

"And if it is all that Nectan claims for it," Conamaill called, "then surely his arguments against Coll's death are just?"

Several other voices called out agreement with this, and with a hand held up to silence them, Domnall looked first at Abiris, and then at Broichan. Abiris told him quietly,

"Nectan has raised questions that demand to be answered, and it seems there should be time taken to discern the will of the gods in this."

"Abiris has spoken well," Broichan agreed. "The issue is clouded, and it might be a mistake to enforce a decision that has no clear sign of approval from the gods."

"An even greater mistake than you imagine!" Niall added loudly, and came thrusting forward as aggressively as Nectan had done. "I can speak fairer on this to you than Nectan can," he told Domnall, "for there has been much bad blood between you two in the past. And I tell you this now, Domnall, that Coll has it in his power to heal the rift that exists between Nectan and yourself; for he has thought of a defense against the raiders that will enable us to stand and fight them as you have always maintained we must—a way that is far more certain of success than any alliance with the Deer or Raven could ever be."

"So that is your aim, is it?" Once more the ranks of the Councillors were broken as Taran burst out from them, furiously shouting. "You think to save the cripple in the same breath as you break the alliance I have worked so hard to make! And to enlist the priests on your side with their woolen-headed debates about the will of the gods. Well, I am a match for you in that—a match for all of you!"

Clapping a hand to the hilt of his sword as he finished speaking, Taran swung around on Domnall. "Why *should* you hesitate to kill him?" he challenged. "He has confessed. He deserves death. So let there be an end to all these priestly scruples about the law. And let there be an end also to all this rambling talk about sunset and golden arrows. Kill him now!"

Domnall's features had hardened at Taran's first slighting reference to the Druids. Now they became grimmer still, and with cold contempt in his voice he observed,

"I know you for what you are, Taran. I have known it from the moment I first guessed you to be lying when you told me about the way you had escaped from slavery. And so do not presume too far on your use to me; for the law is sacred, and so long as I am Chief Druid it shall be applied in every particular. But not until I have dispensed with every doubt over this man's guilt!"

"Doubt!" Taran jeered, and grinned with fierce scorn on the word. "That is something new for you, Domnall! You did not doubt it was right to kill Fand. You did not doubt then that I was your man, and that *my* plans were best!"

"You dare to speak so to *me*!"

Domnall visibly shook with anger as he flung the words at Taran, but Taran himself was too blind with rage now to heed the warning sign.

"I dare to speak as the future ruler of the Boar," he retorted, "which you promised before all these people I should be! I dare to speak as the one man who can enforce unity between them and the other tribes of the islands."

"And what is the reason for this precious, so-called 'unity'?" Domnall snarled. "So that you will become the ruler of the Deer and the Raven as well as Chief of the Boar—is not that your real ambition, Taran? And then you will go on from there, reaching out after the rule of mainland tribes, grasping at power upon power upon power—"

"And who is better fitted to wield such power?" Taran interrupted, shouting. "The Druids, who seek to rule men with ceremonies and pretended mysteries—"

A gasp of horror broke from Abiris and Broichan, and Broichan exclaimed, "This is a godless creature, Domnall!" But recklessly brushing this aside, Taran raged on,

"—or I, Taran, who have seen the Romans show how much better this can be done by force of arms, and who have the will and spirit to follow their example?"

"So I have guessed rightly all along about you, you—you—" Rage choked Domnall so that he could not continue beyond this point, and beginning to splutter in his own rage, Taran shouted,

"But you still would not let yourself believe what you guessed, for you still thought you could control me! You thought the last word would always be with you because your gods were stronger than the war god who has *my* worship! But now know differently, Domnall, for now you endanger my plans. And I will not permit that!"

Domnall's lips clamped shut on his intended reply. His eyes weighed Taran up and down. The passion that had distorted his features hardened again into grimness; and with his own fate forgotten in the tension of the moment, Coll waited breathlessly for the Druid's next words.

The truth was out at last, he thought; and plainly Bran had underestimated Domnall's shrewdness over Taran! But plainly also, Taran had destroyed himself in Domnall's eyes. The old relationship between the two men was finished now, however much either of them might regret the quarrel—or however firmly the Druid thought he could control Taran's ambition. For how could Domnall possibly forgive Taran's public betrayal of their secret dealings? And even more importantly, how could he possibly continue to deal with a man who openly denied the gods, or overlook the blasphemies Taran had uttered?

The silence that had followed the last shouted words stretched cold and brittle as a film of thin ice between Taran and Domnall; then at last, Domnall spoke.

"You will not permit!"

Spacing the sounds out like hammer strokes, Domnall shattered the icy tension. His eyes, fixed on Taran's face, blazed suddenly with the hypnotic power Coll had felt turned on him in the Ring. Taran fell back before the blaze, his right hand straying involuntarily again to his sword hilt; but before he could touch the weapon, Domnall's heavy voice came again.

"See what *I* will not permit!"

His right hand shot out with the words, pointing to Taran's right hand, and the fingers curling toward the sword hilt dropped nervelessly back to Taran's side. Back, and back again he shrank before the blazing eyes, his right arm now hanging apparently useless; and with vengeful triumph Domnall threw after him,

"Seven days and seven nights will you be thus, Taran; your sword arm useless, all strength gone from it. For thus do our gods, the gods of the Boar, permit me to punish your blasphemies against them. Thus do they warn you now of the power you were foolish enough to despise. For thus also do they strike down the soaring black bird of your ambition, and show it to be nothing more than a poor, draggled crow—a carrion eater, a mere scavenger after the eagles it sought to imitate!"

Terror leaped in Taran's face. He tried to raise his right arm again, and failed; then, with beads of sweat starting out on his brow, he brought his left hand up to wrench the deerskin bag off the thong around his neck. One-handed, he fumbled the bag open, and a pebble fell out—a dull, ordinary pebble of sandstone.

"My talisman . . . But where—how—?"

Taran's voice came in a whisper of shocked amazement as he stared down at the pebble; then, whirling toward the wondering faces behind him, he roared,

"Where is it? Where is my talisman—my protection against all harm? Who stole it from me and allowed *this* to happen?"

"You brought evil fortune on yourself!" Domnall's voice rang contemptuously over the echo of his shout; and with his left arm nursing his useless right one, Taran stared in speechless hatred at him.

Coll became aware of Clodha peering toward Taran, a blaze of triumph in her face. He looked away, fearful of directing attention to her, and was relieved to see Niall turning her aside from the sight of Taran stumbling blindly away to the outskirts of the group of Councillors. Those in his path drew aside also, with fearful glances at the evidence of the power Domnall had exerted against him. Nectan spoke rapidly to Niall, but with a wary glance at Taran, Niall appeared to decline the invitation in his words. Nectan shrugged; then, with an air of half expecting a similar fate for his daring, he called out,

"We are not answered yet, Domnall; but we still claim the right to hear Coll speak. And I still claim that he was only a tool of the gods, and cannot therefore be judged guilty of any crime. Moreover, I support Niall's statement that he can heal the quarrel between you and me, for I know he can build a Stronghold that will enable us to stand and fight the raiders as you say we must."

Domnall turned for a final whispered conference with Abiris and Broichan. Coll closed his eyes against the sight, not daring to read his own growing hope into it, but his eyes flew wide open again at the first sound of Domnall's voice.

"Hear me, then," he was answering Nectan. "We must discern the will of the gods in this matter, and this court therefore decides that the prisoner will be allowed to speak to us, and to your Council of Elders. If he can convince us, and them, that the Stronghold Nectan mentions will indeed be all that is claimed for it, this will be a sign that the gods have decided he must be allowed to live—at least until he has had the opportunity of putting his claims to the test. If he cannot so convince us, and at least a majority of your Council, it will equally be a sign that the gods demand his death."

With one hand outflung to Coll, Domnall finished, "Untie the prisoner!" and Niall immediately darted forward to obey the command. Rapidly, as he loosened the knots in the ropes, he whispered encouragement to Coll; but Coll was still struggling with the realization of the test Domnall had imposed, and the whispered words had no meaning for him. With dismay coldly gripping him, he looked from the Druids to the Councillors.

Where was he to start? The Stronghold had been his dream for so long, but how could he ever describe such a dream to all those hard, watching faces? How could he even begin to convince them that his dream could be made reality? Nervously he rubbed at the rope marks on his wrists and then, to his surprise, saw Fand moving toward him.

She was walking purposefully too, he realized, with none of her usual shyness of manner. Head up, her eyes wide with such serious intent that no one—not even Domnall—made any attempt to stop her, she approached and halted beside him. The wide blue eyes rested briefly on him, then she faced toward the rest of the gathering.

"I wish to say something before Coll speaks."

Clear and firm her voice sounded out over the questioning mutter her move had aroused, and the silence of curiosity greeted her words.

"You know well," Fand continued into the silence, "that I have always obeyed the law and observed the customs of the Boar. And you know that I wish to act as the daughter of a Chief should in the matter of my marriage. But this I cannot do, for Coll is the man I wish to marry; and whether he lives or dies now, I declare to you all that I will marry no other."

"No, Fand, no!" Chokingly Coll brought out the denial, turning his head so that Fand would not see the flush of shame on his face. "Please—no pity! Leave me die with *some* pride!"

"But, Coll—" Fand's voice beside him was small and quiet, but he rounded on her as if she had shrieked the words at him.

"It was not for this I saved your life—not so that I could be like a beggar taking a dole of pretended passion from you before *I* died! Or if I am to live, to endure the shame that you should marry me out of an even greater pity!"

"But I do not pity you, Coll. Why should I pity anyone so gifted as you? And I wish you would not keep calling yourself a cripple when you are only a little lame in one leg."

There was a reproving look in the gaze that met his own now, and the gentle voice was becoming insistent.

"Besides which," Fand continued, "do you not remember I have already told you your lameness has never mattered to me? And do you not remember I said that, if things had been different— But I never finished what I had been going to say then, for that was when I thought I was going to die; and it would only have distressed you more if I had told you then that I loved you."

With her voice beginning to shake a little, Fand finished, "Also, I was trying very hard then to behave as a Chief's daughter should, and I had not the courage to speak against the marriage customs. But now I know what it is to face death, and so I know also that this is not so hard as facing life without you."

"I—" Coll began, and stared at her as if he had never seen her before. Fand smiled at him. He whispered her name, then slowly he raised a hand to her face. Gently, as if it were something infinitely delicate that would bruise at a touch, he laid the hand against her cheek, and she smiled again.

"Fand . . . !" He spoke the name aloud, wondering at the sudden music of it; then the harsh voice of Domnall penetrating a clamor of other voices brought his whirling thoughts sharply into focus again.

"—but in the case of a Chief's younger daughter," Domnall's voice bored confidently on, "although there is no absolute law governing her choice of a marriage partner, she is nevertheless still strongly bound by custom. For if it happened that her elder sister should die untimely, then the younger daughter's husband would inherit the position of Chief. Thus, there is a problem in this present case which must be carefully weighed before Nectan and Anu can possibly consider allowing Fand to marry a man who—if he lives to undertake such a marriage—might one day be Chief of the Boar. And how then could the tribe survive with only a cripple to lead them?"

Coll's gaze flew to Nectan and Anu, listening intently to Domnall's words, and his heart bounded in sickening fear at the look that passed between them. They would never allow Fand to marry him, he thought despairingly. Had they not always made that clear—in the kindest way, of course—but still unmistakably clear? Nectan was stepping forward now, his face grave. Coll steadied himself for the blow, and felt Fand's grip on his hand tightening as Nectan said,

"My mind is quite made up on this matter."

He paused, his gaze shifting from Domnall to the two young people facing tensely up to him, then speaking to Coll alone, he said quietly,

"You have never lacked courage. But I see in you also certain qualities of mind which could be of more value to our people than mere physical perfection, and which would better fit you to protect them if you should ever be called upon to succeed to my position. This you have proved to me with your Stronghold. Therefore I give my consent to your marriage with Fand, and if Anu and the Council agree with my judgment on this Stronghold, I call on them to do likewise."

Coll glanced at Fand, and found her smiling. He grinned in reply, a wide uncontrolled grin of incredulous triumph; and wondered briefly why he had ever felt it useless to fight for his life. Turning from her, he found the faces of the Council members crowding in on his vision, and exhilaration mounted in him. This was what he had always wanted—the chance to explain his Stronghold to these men; the chance to convince them of its worth. And to think that now this would also give him the opportunity of winning Fand . . . ! Words formed sharp and clear in his mind, and in tones of crisp authority, he gave them voice.

"We are a people skilled and experienced in the use of stone, and although we live scattered, we have learned to combine our efforts for the common good. Bear this in mind when I speak of my Stronghold, for it will require many men's skill and strength to build. But it will also give us a perfect defense against the raiders, with stone walls that cannot be set on fire; walls so thick that they cannot be undermined, and so high that they cannot be scaled. Also, I have perfected a method of building which will enable us to have at least one such Stronghold ready in time for this season's raiding."

They were giving him their full attention, Coll realized, but there was doubt on some of their faces, and open disbelief on others. Slowly, making every word tell, he continued,

"This Stronghold will be a circular tower of stone set on a solid base, and enclosing a central courtyard. But above this base, it will be a hollow-walled structure with the space between the inner and the outer walls bridged at intervals to create a number of galleries. There will be eight of these galleries, all connected by a staircase winding through each one in turn. Also, the eighth or topmost gallery will be left unroofed for purposes of defense. But mark carefully what I say now."

Coll paused, very aware that he had reached the crucial point of his explanation; then, with even slower and more deliberate emphasis, he continued, "The reason for the hollow-walled structure and the bridging galleries is to do away with the need for wooden scaffolding, *for the roof of each gallery will also be the floor of the one above it.* Thus the galleries will themselves provide all the scaffolding the building needs; and it is this which will enable us to build high—higher than anything ever built on these islands—and faster than we have ever built before."

Now at last, Coll saw, he had broken the barrier of their disbelief! The final words were hardly out of his mouth before a buzz of excited talk broke out among the Councillors, with Taran, Nectan, and Niall at the thick of it; the younger, less experienced men backing Taran's arguments, and the older, wiser ones supporting Niall and Nectan. But it was Anu who caught his attention most strongly, for there was approval as well as surprise in the face she turned toward him now. He glanced at Fand, wondering if she had noticed this encouraging sign, and saw her looking toward the group of Druids.

They were also conferring and their discussion was also an animated one! Domnall turned, as Coll watched them, and moved to him and Fand.

"How did you come to invent this method of building?"

Domnall spoke with a new curiosity in the look he

bent on Coll, and flushing a little at the admission he had to make, Coll told him,

"I am afraid of the raiders. I always have been since—since they crippled me. I wanted to hide from them. Then I realized that hiding was no answer. We had to be able to fight and defend ourselves too. And so I spent my life searching for the perfect way of doing this."

"You have searched to some purpose," Domnall remarked drily. "You can think. You are a discoverer! It may well be that the gods do intend your life to be spared, but we shall see. . . ."

Gartnait's voice came as Domnall turned back to his fellow Druids. "Coll, we cannot decide until we know more about the details of this Stronghold, for Taran has a strong point here when he says that the perfect defense which fails becomes the perfect trap!"

Coll singled out Taran's scowling face from among all the others turned to him, then spoke directly to it, his voice as precise as Gartnait's own.

"The entrance to the Stronghold will be its chief feature of defense, for this will take the form of a passage through the base wall, with a doorway deeply recessed into it. But this passage will be too narrow to permit a team with a battering ram to attack the door itself, and the door will be further secured by a check bar placed across it from the inside."

"And supposing the miracle happens and the door *is* breached?" Taran jeered. "What then, Master Builder?"

"A spear in the ribs for the first enemy through," Coll shot back crisply. "And for each and every one who follows! There will be men stationed in guard cells within the thickness of the base wall on either side of the door's

193

inner face. But supposing the enemy passes even this hazard, he will still have to brave the spears of those stationed at a window opening in the inner wall of each gallery, as well as the weapons raining down on him from the main body of defenders manning the open walls of the topmost gallery. And all before he even sets foot on the first stair into the first of the galleries!"

There was a ripple of laughter at the precision and scope of Coll's retort and Taran's crestfallen expression as he listened to it. Then all eyes turned to the group of Druids as Domnall observed,

"There is one question you have not asked yet, but which will be of prime importance to your decision. Even supposing this young man, Coll, is right when he says you could raise one Stronghold in readiness against the raiders' return this summer, what of all the other settlements that would not be so protected against them?"

"Would these settlements be in any worse case than before?"

Swiftly Nectan countered with his own question, and looked around for support in it. No one openly voiced agreement with his point, but with looks and nods for encouragement, he continued,

"Would there not be a case then for the policy of dispersal which was the original matter of dispute? For a time at least, that is—long enough for us to judge whether a Stronghold for every settlement is indeed the plan we must follow to meet both our own needs and the Druids' commands?"

"A water supply, Coll? Have you thought about a water supply?"

Conamaill called out the question excitedly, with the idea obviously just occurring to him and diverting his mind from the main issue. Half a dozen voices took up the argument it provoked, and with part of his attention still on Nectan and Domnall, Coll tried to answer all the questions that came flying to him out of the argument.

Domnall moved toward Nectan. With heads bent in discussion, the two of them drew a little apart from the rest of the Councillors; and wonderingly Coll realized that this was the first time he had seen these two men talk quietly, without mutual hostility.

Anu began walking toward himself and Fand, a smile on her face. Niall and Clodha followed, smiling also. The rest of the Council drifted after them, still talking and arguing among themselves, still shooting an occasional question at Coll; and looking beyond them he saw that only Ogham and Taran were standing aloof from the general debate.

But these two did not matter now, he told himself, for once Ogham had realized the significance of his own contribution to the day's events, he would forget his resentment and see nothing but the hand of the gods in it. As for Taran, he was nursing the death of all his dreams of power along with that withered arm, for he had no way of enforcing the alliance with Raven and Deer if Domnall was no longer prepared to support him. And for all he had not yet put it into words, it was clear that Domnall had already withdrawn that support.

It was not even necessary to wait for a formal verdict on the outcome of his trial, Coll realized; for that conference between Nectan and Domnall said clearer than words that he had won the battle for his life, and for his Stronghold.

And for Fand! Coll turned to find her smiling up at him. He smiled in reply, and together they raised their clasped hands to receive the touch of Anu's blessing on them.

11
Building

Already the outline of the Stronghold was beginning to dominate the bay!

It stood east of the settlement, on the flat-topped rocky mound that Coll had long ago chosen as the perfect site for it: a great circle of stone wall, twelve feet thick and twelve feet high, with an inside diameter of thirty feet. And although this was only the base from which the galleried part of the walls would rise, it was still enough to indicate the full power of the finished structure.

Coll felt himself dwarfed by it. And yet, he reminded himself, it was his creation. He was Master of the Stronghold. That was the name Nectan had given him before the laying of the very first stone, and all the tremendous organization that had gone into the building so far was his to command! With an unaccustomed feeling of pride in himself, he turned from watching the men who were laying the final course of stones for the base, and looked toward the activity on the beach.

There was his supply of stone—endless quantities of it; an enormous natural storehouse of sandstone shaped by tide and wind and weather to the very kind of blocks and slabs that made for rapid building!

And there, pillaging the storehouse for him now, were men drawn from every settlement in the islands; old men, wise in such matters, skillfully grading the stone to the sizes that would suit each stage in the construction, strong young men laboring over wedges and levers to pry the chosen blocks free; with Gartnait's cool-headed planning directing all their efforts, and Nectan spurring them on with the example of his own sweating back bent constantly to the hardest of the work!

The once-quiet air of the bay was loud now with their shouted directions to one another, and with the yelling and masterful whip-cracking of the boys in charge of the ox teams that pulled the heavy sledgeloads of stone to the building site. And, quiet by contrast, there too were the women and girls of his own settlement, all busily filling rush baskets with the small, flat stones needed for chinking the gaps between the heavier pieces of masonry.

With his eyes traveling over the bent backs of the women and girls, Coll smiled to notice the children who trailed at their heels, with even the smallest child intent on helping to gather the chinking stones. Everyone, he thought gratefully, was making some contribution toward raising his Stronghold—even Taran, in a way, was helping with it!

There was no denying, after all, the hunting skills he had learned from Neith and Drostan; nor that there was a problem in stretching their own food supplies to provide for all the men from those other settlements. And now that Domnall's punishment of him had run its course and he had gained the use of his right hand again, Taran had never been more valuable as a hunter.

With a last glance for the activity centering around Nectan, Coll turned back to his Stronghold. Even more than Gartnait's cool planning, he realized, it was Nectan's example down there on the beach that had brought him thus far with it. And all in less than one moon from the time of his trial at the Guard Stones!

Slowly he paced around the circle of the wall, examining the tightly chinked stonework as he went; then, ducking his head at the beginning of the entrance passage, he moved crouchingly toward the doorway recessed deep within the wall.

Pausing then, with a hand on either jamb of the doorway, he tried to imagine himself a raider caught in this crouching position, with men thrusting spears at him from the guard cells in the thickness of the wall on either side.

There was no defensive stroke possible for a man so positioned, he confirmed and, with cold, hard satisfaction in this conclusion, emerged into the central courtyard. Diagonally facing him now was the door opening that gave access to the stairway beginning within the thickness of the base wall; and still imagining himself as an attacker, he ran toward this opening.

To his left as he entered it, there was a further guard cell that faced to the stairway rising on his right; and standing ready to mount this stair, Coll argued the attacker's point of view to himself. If *he* were rushing to climb a stairway that rose on his right, he decided, he would never think to glance first toward his left; and so he would never even notice the guard cell recessed into the wall on his left side. And that would mean death for him the moment he mounted the first step, for to do that he would have to turn his back on the spears of the men hidden in the guard cell.

"We are almost ready to begin building the first gallery, Coll!"

A voice calling down the stairway jerked him back to the present moment, and sent him hurrying to find out whether Niall had arrived to direct the part he would play in this operation. The figure he could see coming up from the beach, however, turned out to be Taran; and to his annoyance, Taran brought most unwelcome news with him.

"Anu says her food supplies are running so short that you will have to release more men for the hunt," Taran announced; and as Coll stared in dismay at this, he added truculently, "And I agree with her. We have already had one man badly wounded by a boar; and on the seal hunt yesterday, there was another of us who suffered a broken arm."

Coll looked toward the beach. "Pick the two men you want, then," he said curtly. "Ask Gartnait's permission to release them from the work there; but tell Gartnait also that he must still manage to send up the same quantity of stone—as *I* will manage to keep up the rate of building here."

Taran ran curious eyes over the wall towering massively above them. "How will you do that?" he asked. The curious glance came back to Coll. "What *do* you do here all day, every day?"

There was a jeering note in the questions. But there

had been something else too, Coll realized. Taran's voice had betrayed envy; a loser's envy. And it would be ungenerous not to make allowance for such a feeling. Carefully keeping his own voice on an even tone, he answered,

"Only what I have planned every day for the last thirteen years to do. I watch the laying of stone upon stone to make each course. I plan the line of the courses as they ascend, and the amount of overlap each one should have to create the curve the wall must take. And presently, I shall be judging the height the walls of each gallery must reach before the inner wall is bonded to the outer one by the flagstones forming the roof of that gallery. In a word, Taran, I direct the building of my Stronghold. And because all the men here have learned that I make no mistakes in this, they work for me as well and as quickly as it is possible for men to work."

Taran stared at him. "You are so sure it will be all you have claimed for it," he remarked. "I wondered about that—wondered how you could be so sure."

"And now perhaps you understand why," Coll told him. "With thirteen years of planning behind me, Taran, I can afford to be sure."

"Coll—" Taran moved a step nearer, his eyes gleaming with the light of a sudden idea. "Have you thought about this? If your first Stronghold *is* a success, and if you build one for each settlement as you have planned, the whole islands would owe their safety to you! The people would all look up to you then, the Raven and the Deer as well as the Boar. And that would give you great power, Coll—greater than any Chief of any tribe."

"You have misread my character, Taran. I am not interested in power."

With cold dislike, Coll returned the gleaming glance directed at him, but still Taran persisted,

"Ah, but you have not understood, Coll. The Romans will come here in force someday; to conquer the islands, not simply to raid for slaves. I have already warned you of that—remember? They will come with a whole fleet, not simply a few vessels, and they will bring a great army, with terrible engines of war that can knock down even your strong defenses. But if you were master of the islands by that time—as you could be, if you took advantage of the power your Strongholds will bring you—you could make a bargain with them! The kind of bargain, Coll, that would leave the people only a very little worse off in some ways than they are now, and much better off in other ways!"

Coll hesitated, repelled by the eager cunning in Taran's face, yet was curious in spite of himself; and asked cautiously,

"How could that be?"

"Oh, very simply." Taran spoke with the airy confidence of a man well versed in such diplomacy.

"The kind of bargain I mean is one they have agreed before to make with territories that are distant from their center of power, and so troublesome to administer. It would require you only to make some sort of formal submission to them, and to pay them a yearly tribute—in slaves, of course, since that is the prize they want from the islands. In return for which, they would not only leave you in peaceful possession here, they would also give you any help you needed to hold your position. Just think of the advantages of that, Coll! No more raids. No more of the tribe's best blood lost to the Romans—for of course, you would select whom you wanted to be given in tribute. You could even breed them especially for that purpose, if necessary!"

"And who would make this treaty for us? Who would bargain with the Romans?"

For all the shocked incredulity that had invaded his mind by this time, Coll managed to say this in his normal voice, but an edge of sarcasm he could not disguise crept into it as he continued,

"You, Taran? The only one of us who knows their language? Is that what you are aiming for? But you are an escaped slave, a fugitive from Roman justice. How could you speak for us?"

"Easily!" Taran's lips gave the cruel twist that passed for a smile with him. "I am no fugitive, Coll. I never was! Nor have I ever killed a Roman. I was slave to a Roman woman who was fool enough to give me my freedom; but I knew how useful the Druids could be to me here, and how they hate the Romans. And that was why I deceived Domnall with the tale of killing my Roman master."

"Deceived more than Domnall!" Coll exclaimed. "Everything you told us was also a lie!"

"Not everything," Taran protested. "Not the tale of that terrible voyage. Nor the finding of my talisman. That was real enough. And the luck it brought me was real."

Taran's face clouded momentarily as he spoke of his vanished carnelian; then, recollecting his purpose, he pressed on,

"And so you see, Coll, I *could* speak for you, and be your right-hand man in making such a bargain."

"Only to kill me eventually, and take my place!"

The shock and disgust Coll had felt showed openly in his voice now, and holding up a hand to silence the protest Taran would have made, he continued,

"Learn this, Taran, and learn it finally. I mean it when I say that *I am not interested in power*. I agree with Nectan that we will meet the threat of a Roman invasion when it comes—if it ever does come. And finally, no one from the tribe of the Boar will be sold into slavery while *I* live—"

"But they would be simple people," Taran protested. "Poor field workers—bondsmen, who are little better than slaves as it is—"

"But still Men of the Boar!" Coll interrupted in his turn, "and therefore of one blood with me and all the other tribesmen of the Boar. You understand nothing till you have understood that, Taran. And so, go now. Ask Gartnait for the two hunters you need, and either learn to live by *our* rules or leave us altogether. We did without you before you returned here, and we can still do so."

The eagerness drained from Taran's face, and was replaced by a curiously hunted look. One hand strayed to the little bag that had once held his carnelian, and uncertainly he said,

"I—well, it was a thought that struck me. But I— It seems I have no luck with anything since my carnelian was stolen—I do not know how. I . . ."

The uncertain voice trailed into silence. But Coll did not stay to hear what else might be said; for now he could see Niall coming up from the beach, and so it was time to sling the ropes for hoisting the needed sledgeloads of stone up to the first gallery. Impetuously he brushed past Taran, and so missed the return of cunning to the other's face, and the look of bitter hostility that followed him as he limped forward to hail Niall.

With a vision of the completed gallery in his mind, he followed his shout to Niall with a series of rapid instructions to the men who would be operating the rope hoists, and had neither time nor inclination to think of Taran again until that night when he and Niall were alone in their quarters. But Niall, he discovered, was inclined to laugh at the fears the recollection of his conversation with Taran aroused in him then.

"Taran is finished, and he knows it," Niall told him cheerfully. "He knew it as soon as Domnall turned against him. But even then, it took the loss of his carnelian to convince him his luck had changed; and this scheme he put to you was only a last dying flicker of his ambition."

Coll suddenly remembered Clodha savagely pounding the carnelian to dust; and shivered at the thought of the death wish behind the hatred in her face then. Niall spoke again, before finally turning over for sleep.

"Forget Taran, Coll," he advised. "Put him out of your mind altogether. It is the measure of his lack of judgment now that he even proposed such a scheme to you. But you answered him plainly enough, and there is nothing more he can try."

And Taran lacked judgment now, Coll thought, because he had lost confidence in himself when he lost his precious talisman. That was what Bran had intended should happen—Bran, slim and white and pumping red blood into the sunlight of sacrifice. . . . Bran, the child of destiny shaping their lives still from somewhere in the Otherworld. . . .

But Bran had not expected Clodha to destroy the carnelian. He had not willed the ritual death she had enacted; pounding, pounding at the carnelian. . . . Clodha would not forget Taran; not till he was safely, finally dead. . . .

Coll sank into sleep with the faces of Taran, Clodha, and Bran drifting in a confused blur through his mind; and woke from an uneasy night, resolved to follow Niall's advice. Taran's fangs were drawn, after all, he reminded himself, and he was no more of a menace now than a jealous, toothless dog snapping on the outskirts of the real battle—which was to have the Stronghold ready against the first attack of the raiders.

Much to his annoyance that day, however, work on the first gallery slowed down for lack of a quick supply of chinking stone. Then Niall came to the rescue with a gang of agile small boys keeping a hand-to-hand chain of baskets passing up the inside stair; with another and even more agile gang of children catching the empty baskets thrown down to them, and racing back to the women for fresh supplies.

Yet still Coll raged at the delay. And driving everyone the harder for it, he gradually lengthened the work schedules until they covered every hour in the long daylight period that summer had brought to the northerly latitude of the islands.

Now, he knew, he *was* pushing every man, woman, and child to the limit of endurance; but to his relief and unbounded gratitude, the solidarity of the Boar stood up even to this test. Children fell asleep where they worked, men and women sagged with fatigue, yet nobody rebelled. No one even grumbled. The growing height of the Stronghold, it seemed, was reward enough for those long, backbreaking days, and with every gallery that was added to it, the speed of the work improved.

Gartnait kept up an unceasing procession of ox teams with stone from the beach. Niall's routine of hoisting the sledgeloads to the workers in the galleries became smooth and fast. And early on in this frantic spurt of effort, Anu made another saving in time. There must be no more hours wastefully consumed in family cooking, she decreed. Then casting off all dignity, as Nectan had done, she led the women in digging a long communal hearth on the beach, and herself presided every evening over the food prepared there.

Coll joined the gathering around this fire each evening, almost too tired to think; and sometimes as he took his place quietly there beside Fand, he had the strangest sense of having entered a scene witnessed many times before. Or was it only because he had dreamed of it so often—this gray dusk made friendly by firelight, this shared food that was like a small festival of thankfulness to the gods; those faces, tired and dusty, the faces of his fellow tribesmen all mustered to the building of his Stronghold, all eagerly convinced at last that they had the answer to the raiders' attacks. . . .

"But an answer only on certain terms!"

The sound of Nectan's voice, adding a warning note to his thoughts, jerked Coll sharply to attention one evening when near-completion of the fifth gallery had channeled conversation toward the actual manning of the Stronghold. Leaning forward to where Nectan sat hunched over his food, he listened intently to the deep voice rumbling on,

"We cannot pick and choose among all those here for

warriors to man the Stronghold against the first attack. Remember that, for that was the heart of the agreement with Domnall. To make a fair test of its worth to any settlement, it must be defended only by the men of this particular one."

Gartnait's eyes flickered to Taran. "Then you will need every man you have, Nectan," he remarked dryly.

"Of course." Briefly, Nectan followed Gartnait's glance. "But do you see any here who would be unwilling to fight?"

There was a second of silence, with the question still hovering in the air; then, raising his eyes to meet Gartnait's glance full on, Taran asked calmly,

"Or any who would not bring a man's full strength to the battle?"

Gartnait frowned, as if suspecting some hidden meaning in the question, but Nectan apparently had no such doubts now.

"So," he said briskly. "We can count on every man of the settlement to play his part. But there is another thing I must tell you, which is this. *I* shall not captain the fighting from the Stronghold. That will be Niall's task, for he has worked so closely with Coll over it that he knows all its possibilities. Besides which, the Stronghold is our defense of the future, and the future belongs to young men."

There was a brief, surprised silence, followed by an enthusiastic shout from all the young men around Nectan, and a more cautious approval from the older men.

"But I shall be there to advise Niall, of course." Smiling slightly as he added this further warning note, Nectan turned to the older men and added,

"Thus, you see, I take my decision on this from the

custom of the Boar; for so it must also be when Niall marries Clodha—the young Chief to lead you, the old one to remain on his Council and advise him."

"But you have not yet obtained the consent of the Council to Niall's marriage with Clodha, and such a transfer of power is not lawful until you do."

It was Ogham who had raised the objection. Coll felt a surge of impatience as he recognized the melancholy tones, then, glimpsing the face that peered toward Nectan, was relieved to see there was no hostility in it. True to form, he told himself, Ogham was simply anxious to see the gods were not offended! And Nectan, it seemed, was prepared to be reasonable with him, for his reply came mildly enough.

"I am sure the Councillors here will agree that is a mere formality, Ogham. Nevertheless, let them all observe it now, and give me their decision."

"You have my consent, Nectan."

Gartnait spoke up crisply. Conamaill followed him; and their consent was echoed by three others and finally by Ogham himself. Nectan's eyes searched further among those seated by the fire, and rested briefly on Taran. But Taran's consent was not necessary now, Coll realized. With these six votes to add to his own, Nectan had already obtained a majority decision, and Taran had recognized this. The shrug he gave, the carefully continued blankness of his expression, were his way of acknowledging the situation.

"So it is settled!" Nectan spoke triumphantly, and Niall rose to his feet on the words, a broad grin lifting the tiredness from his dusty face, fair head handsomely gleaming in the firelight. Nectan came to stand shoulder to shoulder with him, and Anu rose also, leading a smiling Clodha forward with her.

From all sides then, a pleased murmur arose as Nectan joined Clodha's hand to that of Niall; and for once, Coll was almost sorry for Taran, for now no amount of self-control could hide the chagrin he felt. Nectan's voice came again, however, quelling the cheer and the moments of celebration that threatened to sharpen even further the sting of Taran's discomfiture.

"I have not finished yet," he announced, "for I have still to tell you that we cannot risk taking the women and children into the Stronghold with us until we have proved that we can indeed hold it successfully against all attacks. At the first sign of the raiders, therefore, all the women and children must flee inland—"

"Not all of them!" Her voice sharp as a whipcrack, Clodha interrupted Nectan, and faced him defiantly. "I shall stay by Niall's side, and fight beside him if I am called upon to fight."

"You will not!" Indignantly Niall turned on her, forestalling Nectan's own attempt at reply. "You could be *killed*, girl! You have—"

"I have rights!" Clodha interrupted so fiercely that Niall recoiled from her and even Nectan looked taken aback. "I am the future mother of the Boar, and it is my right to stand in battle beside the man chosen for my husband!"

"But Clodha—" Nectan tried a gentler approach. "Supposing you *are* killed? What will become of the Boar then?"

"You will still have Fand," Clodha told him stubbornly. "She will be safe enough in the usual hiding place."

"No, Clodha!"

To Coll's amazement, it was Fand who spoke up next, and as he turned to stare at her she continued,

"I shall go with the other women and their children, for they might well meet with a raiding party of the Raven or the Deer when they fly inland. And how could I continue selfishly in safety when even children may have to face such dangers?"

"Have I gone mad? Or have *you* both gone mad?" Staring from one stubborn face to the other, Nectan beat his fists against his forehead, and then turned to appeal to Anu,

"Anu, speak to your daughters; convince them they must go into hiding with you. Show them the risks they propose to take!"

Anu shook her head. "I cannot do that, Nectan. No one can dispute the right Clodha claims now."

Nectan's mouth opened, fishlike, in astonishment. Then, helplessly glaring at Anu, he exploded,

"And what about Fand? Our warrior numbers are few, Anu—too few to spare anyone but old men and boys to protect the women's flight. And how *could* I trust Fand's safety to so feeble and leaderless a company?"

Anu stared in silence at him. Then, still without turning her head, she commanded, "Someone—quickly! Give me a sword!"

There was a stir and a mutter around the fire, then a hand came up, reaching out a sword to Anu. She grasped it and, leaning its point on the ground, looked about the forms crouched by the fire. Her eye rested on the flaming red head of the boy Ibar.

"Ibar, son of Echu," she commanded, "come stand by me."

Ibar unscrambled his lanky form, and hastened to obey. Anu laid her free hand on the bony, boyish shoulder beside her, and faced Nectan again.

"Think back over the years," she told him, "to the time I claimed the right that Clodha claims now. I proved then that the women of my line can match any man in battle, and therefore *I* shall lead the guard of the women's party. I shall reawaken the courage of the old men, Nectan; give even poor bondsmen swords to wield, turn boys like this into noble warriors. And it will be no feeble company then that protects Fand!"

Coll began rising from his place by the fire. There might be further arguments, he realized. Nectan might bluster and protest before he finally accepted the situation; but Anu and Clodha had custom on their side, and in the tribe of the Boar, custom always had the last word. The matter was already settled, and so there was nothing now to stop him taking his final, nightly look at the Stronghold.

Fand had sensed the purpose of Coll's movement and was rising with him. He grasped her hand, drawing quietly away with her from the renewed sound of voices, then plunged with quickening pace into the darkness. The outline of the Stronghold loomed ahead of them, and wordlessly ignoring the events by the fireside, he hurried Fand toward it.

They reached the entrance passage, and Coll checked their progress, the better to savor the excitement that penetrating to the heart of his own creation always aroused in him. Then, ducking his head, he led their crouching way into the central courtyard.

Standing there with Fand at his side, he sent a practiced eye roving to the highest part of the surrounding walls. With only the height of three more galleries to build, he reckoned, it would take less than a moon to complete the Stronghold now. But even if the raiders came before that time it would be possible to hold it against them.

The cesspit had been dug. They had their water supply led in through an underground channel starting far back in the course of the stream that watered the settlement— too far back for the raiders to discover the point at which the stream had been tapped. There was a hearth prepared for the fire of Echu, the smith, and his tools lay beside it, ready to carry out any necessary work on their weapons.

"It feels so peaceful here!" Fand spoke almost in a whisper as she craned her head to look upward at the heavy walls towering over them. "So quiet and peaceful, Coll. And so wonderfully *safe*!"

"I know. I know exactly what you mean, Fand."

Coll answered in the same whispering tones, his gaze rising from the doorway of the staircase and tracing above it the vertical line of the openings that pierced the inner wall of each gallery. The openings ended at the fifth and last of the galleries, and still craning up to that point, he began turning slowly round and around on his heel so that the whole towering height of the wall encircling himself and Fand seemed also to turn, spinning slowly like a monstrous wheel through the starry dark above it. And slowly, in time to his own turning, Coll chanted,

"*Safe . . . Quite, quite safe . . . Here—I—feel—fear— is not—real. . . .*"

"Coll!" Laughing, Fand caught him as he staggered

213

dizzily and almost fell. "Is this why you come here every night?" she teased. "To play games like a child?"

"In a way," Coll told her quietly. "In a way. I have been here in fancy from the time I was a child—remember?"

Fand nodded, and there was silence between them for a few moments; then, still without speaking, Coll set off on his usual tour of inspection. With fingers tracing the stone and telling him what darkness hid from his eyes, he climbed up the stair winding through each of the galleries, and stood looking out over the bay from an unroofed section of the fifth gallery.

That turning around on his heel had been a stupid business, he told himself. It had pained his lame leg, and now his heart was hammering from the climb up the steeply circling stairs. Yet still he grinned to himself in the darkness, for the rapid pounding of his heart was beating out the message that soon, soon, the Stronghold would be finished!

Soon, soon, the last of the galleries would be raised; and when Domnall came to inspect the completed work, as he had sent to tell Nectan he would, he would understand at last the full measure of the test on which the trial of the sacrilegious cripple had turned!

To build a dream in stone—that had been the challenge thrown at Coll the cripple! To save his life with the dream . . . Domnall had not known it, Coll told himself, but *that* had been the true meaning of the terms he had set to the test!

The wind blew coldly at that height from the ground. Yet it was still a clear night that promised a clear dawning. Coll turned his back on the wind, blessing the lucky chance that had kept the changeable weather of the islands so settled over the past weeks and thus provided yet another factor in favor of the work's rapid progress.

With a critical eye for the line of the supports for the opening in the inner wall of the fifth gallery, he advanced toward the windowlike space and, glancing down into the central courtyard, saw Fand standing with her head craned up toward him.

She looked tiny, standing there by herself at the center of such a massive creation. And very lonely, somehow. Coll's heart smote him for having left her so long alone, and turning back to the stairway, he hurried down to her again. Fand spoke as he came toward her.

"Coll—I wish . . ." her voice shook, and she stopped speaking. Coll felt a flush of alarm, and asked quickly,

"Fand, what is it? Are you afraid, after all, to go with the rest of the women? Would you rather hide, as you have always done before? You can still do that, Fand. Indeed, I would rather have it that way. It would be safer, and there is no need—"

"No, no, Coll!" Impatiently Fand stemmed the rush of his words. "It is not that. I shall be perfectly safe with Anu playing the warrior, and devoted hearts like Ibar to protect me!"

Coll stared at her. "Are you mocking Ibar, Fand?" he asked quietly. "That is not fair. He is but young, of course; but there is nothing comic about his devotion, for it has helped once before to save your life."

"I know. And I am not mocking him. I am grateful to him, but—" Fand's voice faltered to a stop again, and then she burst out, "—but he is not *you*, Coll! And I wish—oh, I wish I were like Clodha. I wish I were strong and brave enough to stay here and fight with you!"

"Fand, listen!" Reaching out to lay his hands on her shoulders, Coll drew her gently close to himself.

"Listen to what my Stronghold has always meant to me. All my remembered life I have been a cripple among a people who worship strength and comeliness. All I have ever had was my dream of building the Stronghold. But that dream was itself a stronghold to me, Fand; for nothing could destroy it, no enemy could take it from me. I lived safe and secure inside my dream. For me, it was the strength and comeliness I have always lacked. It was perfect, and it would last forever."

Fand was trembling under his hands. Her face looking up at him was a pale flowering in the darkness. Coll felt himself beginning to shake with the strength of the emotion that gripped him, and had to force steadiness into his voice as he continued,

"But you were never inside that dream of mine, Fand, for I never dared to let myself hope that you could love me. *And I do not want you there now.* For if you should be killed in the fighting here, as Clodha may be killed, I shall not want to live. But once my Stronghold has proved itself beyond any possibility of doubt, you *shall* step into my dream, into my Stronghold, and be always safe and secure there with me. And secret too, Fand; for no one will ever know that here, in the heart of the Stronghold, we two are also in the very heart of my dream. No one but you and I, Fand. No one . . ."

Silence—a long silence; then Fand leaned toward him, and his arms were around her, holding her close. Fand's face was pressed against him, and her voice came, muffled,

"But you might be killed, Coll. . . ."

"*Never!*" Coll shouted, the gentle pressure of his arms tightening to a sudden bear hug on the sound. Fand squealed at the shock of it and, gasping with indignation, fought to free herself.

"Never, never, never!" Laughing as he controlled her threshing arms, Coll chanted the words. "Do you hear that, Fand? You will be safe with Anu, and I shall not be killed. Never, never, never!"

Fand stopped struggling to gape in amazement at him, and exclaimed,

"Coll, you are laughing! You are laughing out loud—*you*, Coll!"

Bewilderment silenced her momentarily, then she blundered on, "But you *never* laugh out loud!"

"I never have laughed out loud," Coll corrected her. "But I shall now, Fand. I shall now! For I need not fear to laugh now, *and* I have cause to do so. To dance too, if I please, for why should I care now if I am lame? I have my dream, and I have you. I am Master of the Stronghold now, Fand, *and I have you!*"

With his voice rising to a shout again on the last words, Coll whirled Fand off her feet and, roaring with renewed laughter at his own limping efforts, danced wildly with her; back and forward, round and round. . . . The first dance he had ever danced; the first dance of war and love and triumph inside his Stronghold.

12
Battle

The raiders came on a day of brass-bright sunshine, when even the tormenting wind of the islands had dropped to a breeze that barely ruffled the bay. And as luck would have it, that day was also the one when the last of the helpers from other settlements had departed, and Domnall had come on his promised visit to inspect the completed Stronghold.

Coll and Nectan were with him in the topmost gallery when the lookout on the headland sounded his warning trumpet call; and from this high vantage point, they saw the empty peace of the settlement so suddenly transformed that the very ground itself seemed to have thrown up the scurrying mass of figures.

The mass resolved into two streams—one of men racing for the Stronghold, the other of women and children hurrying to cross the ridge behind the settlement. The boys and grandfathers and bondsmen of Anu's motley army moved on the sidelines of the women's flight, helping with the children, lending an arm to support any who could not keep the general pace. Anu herself gained the crest of the ridge before anyone else, and beckoned the women on from there with one hand, while the other imperiously pointed her sword in the direction they must take.

Coll's gaze scanned this orderly haste until it lighted on Fand laboring over the ridge with a small child in her arms; but Nectan withdrew quickly from his first appraisal of the situation, and said in urgent tones,

"Hurry, Domnall! There is time for you to join the women's flight, and your presence will comfort them."

"I do not doubt that." Domnall drew himself up, bristling with offended dignity. "But it is no part of the Chief Druid's duty to comfort women when there are warriors to be encouraged in battle and an enemy to curse. I stay here, Nectan!"

The Stronghold was beginning to resound with voices as men took up the positions allotted to them there. Coll lost Nectan's reply in the noise of feet pounding up the stairs to the top gallery, but had the feeling that lack of time to argue meant that Nectan's attempt to get rid of Domnall had already failed. Which was a pity, he concluded, for men inflamed to blind courage by Domnall's battle frenzies would certainly be more of a hindrance than a help in the cautious tactics of defensive fighting!

The exit from the stairs began to give out a steady stream of men, and turning from it, Coll stared seaward. The bay was still an empty, dancing ripple of blue water, but already the old familiar pounding of his heart had begun. Already he could feel his mouth dry, and the sweat starting out on the palms of his hands. Another pair of hands came out to rest beside his own on the chest-high parapet of the gallery—Niall's hands, and he became aware of Niall and Clodha standing at his side.

Clodha's dress was warrior dress—a shoulder cloak, and a tunic short to the knee. Her hair was no longer plaited in woman's style, but flowing free from under the same kind of bronze fillet that bound Niall's long fair locks. She had a sword belted round her waist, a javelin in her right hand, a shield on her left arm. Both she and Niall were panting, as much with excitement as with their rush up the stairs, and it struck Coll that he had never seen them so magnificently matched as in the shared ardor of that moment.

With a nod of acknowledgment to their greeting, he glanced around at the rest of the main defense force now also standing ready for action, then turned to ask Niall quietly,

"Is that everyone safely in, then?"

"How can you be so calm!" Niall met his glance with a look of wondering admiration, then nodded. "Yes, everyone. Except for the lookout, of course; but he should have time to reach us before the raiders land."

Coll looked back toward the blue dance of the bay's waters, and did not answer. Niall's admiration was a ludicrous mistake, he thought bleakly, for he was not really calm. He was simply numb with terror! And presently that terror would explode in his mind; presently, when the raiders' vessels were sighted. . . .

They rounded the headland, two of them, shooting black and huge out of the sun's eye: the single square sail on each one barely filled by the breeze, the banks of oars rising and falling in long, rhythmic sweeps. The drumbeat that timed the oars sounded faintly over the distance separating them from the shore, and from the deck of each long black shape came the gleam of helmeted heads and shoulder armor shifting in the sun's rays.

Nightmare seized Coll by the throat again: the daytime nightmare of a hand twisted cruelly in his hair, a grinning face level with his own, a shining orb of helmet nodding over the face—*space beneath him—his mother's voice screaming—a breathless, twisting rush through air—pain, brutally piercing as he struck the rocks....*

Through the panic in his mind he clutched at a vision of the door of his Stronghold, and was astonished to hear his own voice sounding perfectly normal as he said,

"Time to see if the lookout is safely with us, Niall."

Without waiting for an answer to this, he turned to the parapet of the gallery's inner wall. Some of the ropes the builders had used for hoisting stone up to that height lay at his feet there, and quickly grappling one to the inner parapet, he climbed over to slide down into the central courtyard.

As Coll's feet touched the ground there, the lookout man stumbled in, panting from his run down from the headland. The men in the guard cells to left and right of the inner side of the doorway began heaving on the levers needed to raise the great stone slab of the door itself into position. With a dull, grinding thud the door slab was forced home against its supporting jambs, and suddenly, at this sound, Coll found he was the master builder again and no longer afraid.

It was too slow and clumsy a process to have that door slab levered into position, he thought critically; and the answer to that would be to have it hinged to one jamb so that it could be swung quickly into place. The thick wooden check bar behind the door was slotted into the sockets prepared for it, and satisfied that the entrance was now completely secure, he hurried to the stairway.

The guard cell facing onto the stairs was a narrow cavern of dimness, and the men stationed within it almost invisible even to Coll's experienced glance. Rapidly he climbed the fifteen steps winding up to the first gallery, where the light from the window opening showed the readiness of the men poised there, with spears directed at the inner face of the door closing the entrance passage.

On then, round and up through the succeeding six galleries, each one with its determined knot of warriors at the window looking into the courtyard; each one, Coll's hurrying thoughts told him, an ideal refuge for the women and children once the coming battle had finally tested the Stronghold and proved it impregnable. On, and out into the open air of the eighth gallery, with brilliant sunshine hitting him again so suddenly that he was momentarily blinded, and Niall's voice urgently summoning him,

"Coll, look here! They have landed!"

The raiders had not only landed, they were already fanning out to reconnoiter the deserted settlement. The man who seemed to be the commander of their force stood directing this operation, and Coll heard Nectan say quietly to Niall,

"Keep your eyes on that stick their commander carries. It is his wand of office, and the signals he makes with it will warn you of each stage in the attack."

Niall nodded acknowledgment of the advice, then frowned at the sound of another voice shouting,

"Clear a way there for me, Men of the Boar! A cry, the cry of war is rising in me!"

Domnall came thrusting aggressively forward with the words, all ready to mount the gallery's outer parapet and lead the howling war cry of the Boar; but Niall laid a firm, restraining grip on his arm and said curtly,

"No, old man, this will not be your kind of fighting. Leave us the cool heads we shall need for it."

Domnall's face sagged in astonishment, then swiftly recovering himself, he snarled, "And who do you think you are—a cub like you—to talk so to *me*?"

"The commander of the Stronghold," Niall threw back at him. "And any man who disobeys me—*any* man—will be tossed over the wall to the Romans!"

Moving swiftly away then for another glance over the outer parapet, he surveyed the Roman force now withdrawing from the settlement to form a wide circle around the Stronghold and some seventy-five yards distant from it.

"A hundred of them to our forty," he observed quietly to Coll, then turning inward to face his own force, he shouted,

"The Romans will begin by trying to draw us, but we shall be fighting on the defensive, and *no man will offer himself as a target to them*. Keep down behind the parapet of the gallery when I tell you to keep down. Now—"

The Roman commander had his stick raised in some sort of signal. Niall broke off his speech to watch intently for its next movement, and as the stick came flashing back to the officer's side, he yelled,

"*Down!*"

Coll ducked along with everyone else to crouch below the level of the parapet, and felt a tremor of amusement as he saw that Domnall had also ducked to cover. There was a high, whining sound from a flight of arrows flashing over the parapet to pass harmlessly above their heads, and Niall called,

"Keep down! It will be javelins next!"

A brief pause, then the javelins skimmed in twisting flight over the parapet and plunged down into the courtyard. Niall gazed upward with a critical eye for this second attempt to probe the Stronghold's defenses; and reading his thoughts, Coll said,

"But the next flight of javelins will be covering fire for a party trying to test the strength of the door!"

Niall nodded, and cautiously began rising erect. Coll followed his example and saw the circle of Roman soldiers re-forming so that all of them were faced toward the point where he stood with Niall, and thus also toward the entrance passage directly below their position.

"Door coming under attack!" Niall yelled, and stepped back instantly to allow room for Finn and Becuma, the two strongest among the young warriors of Nectan's household. Finn bent to a pile of boulders lying in readiness and, choosing one that was twice the size of a man's head, heaved it up to rest on the parapet. Becuma followed suit, and the two men crouched side by side with hands advanced to steady the boulders lying in front of them.

Coll snatched up the shield Becuma had discarded, and masking head and shoulders with it, leaned out over the parapet. Standing at Finn's side, and using his own shield in similar fashion, Niall also leaned out. The Roman commander's stick signaled the next phase of the attack, and six of his men began making a dash for the entrance to the Stronghold.

Crouchingly and in close two-by-two formation they ran. Their shields, raised and held flat overhead to form a single, interlocking shield, gave them the appearance of a gigantic beetle scurrying along; and from the main party behind them came a hail of javelins to cover the beetle's rush. One javelin after another struck sharply against the shields held by Coll and Niall; but each clung grimly to his watch on the beetle's rate of progress, for together they had worked out the exact correlation of this with the speed at which the boulders would drop.

The twisting flight of a javelin ended with the weapon's point embedded in the exposed flesh of Becuma's left forearm. He swore, but held steadily to his boulder. The head of the beetle reached the required distance from the actual point of impact. Coll snapped, *"Now!"* and Becuma heaved his boulder over the parapet.

It dropped straight onto the interlocked shields of the two leading runners, smashing both shields and men down with its impact. The men blindly following crashed into the fallen leaders, and as the beetle broke into a tangled heap of men and shields, Niall roared,

"And again!"

Finn heaved his boulder down onto the heap of fallen, shouting bodies. Becuma followed immediately with another. Then it was Finn's turn again, and the pattern was remorselessly continued until there was only one Roman crawling out alive from the wreckage below. Becuma snatched at the haft of the javelin still embedded in his forearm and took aim at the figure staggering dazedly away from the entrance, but Niall stayed his action and said quickly,

"No! Leave that one alive!"

"Leave a Roman alive when you have the chance to kill him?"

Domnall's voice came in shocked protest from farther along the gallery, but Niall did not answer, and it was Nectan who explained patiently,

"One man left alive to report will be able to tell how low and narrow the door entrance is. And that will save us at least one form of further attack, for their commander will then know there is no room to swing a battering ram against the door."

The Roman commander was now dispatching some of his men back toward the raiding craft. Coll turned to watch them, trying to guess at the purpose behind the move, and saw that two other vessels had appeared in the bay and were riding at anchor beyond the beached craft.

The newcomers were larger and squatter than the narrow craft which had sped the soldiers ashore—merchantmen of the kind the raiders used to transport their slave cargoes—and nodding toward them, he remarked to Niall,

"There are no slaves as yet aboard their transport vessels, Niall, or they would not ride so high in the water. We must be the first settlement to receive their attack!"

"Ye-e-e-s." Niall spoke thoughtfully, his gaze shifting from the party dispatched shoreward to the officer waiting with his command stick. "But what will they try now, Coll? Scaling ladders? Is that what these men have been sent to fetch?"

"Of course not," Coll began, and stopped short as he recognized what the men of the shore-to-ship party were manhandling on to the beach. Niall stared past him at the two sections of timber, each crosspieced with steps nailed on at every foot of its thirty-foot length.

"Of course not!" he repeated scornfully. "Then what are these? And *you* said they would never even attempt an attack with scaling ladders!"

"And I still say that!" Coll returned angrily. "The height—"

"You keep talking about the height of the Stronghold," Niall interrupted. "But what is to stop the Romans splicing these two lengths to make one ladder that *is* long enough to reach this gallery?"

"Niall!" Nectan was on his feet, shouting, and stabbing a finger toward the ladder party now rejoining their main group. Niall nodded grim acknowledgment of the warning, and turned to shout,

"Stand ready, all. They may be preparing to scale the Stronghold!"

Domnall was the first to spring to his feet, but with one eye on Niall, Nectan managed to dissuade him from a renewed attempt at cursing the enemy. Finn and Becuma formed the beginning of a chain that passed boulders from hand to hand, until the entire circumference of the outer parapet was edged with them. Clodha took up a determined stand at Niall's shoulder, her sword so competently at the ready that a passing glance would have assumed her to be one with all the other young warriors looking toward the point where—as Niall had feared would happen—the Romans were now busy splicing the two ladders in preparation for a scaling attempt.

But it was all a blind. There could not be such an attempt!

With the anger of frustration surging in his mind, Coll stared at the sixty-foot ladder the Romans were constructing from the two thirty-foot lengths, and wondered how he could possibly explain the problems of leverage they would face in raising it to the height of the top gallery. But explain he must, he realized, for apparently no one but himself could see the real purpose behind all this activity!

"Niall—!" Urgently he caught at the other's arm. "The height of the Stronghold *will* make this impossible for them. I know I am right about that, and you must listen."

"I am listening," Niall said, but his attention was still on the Romans and the almost-completed result of their efforts.

"It is simply not possible to lift a ladder of that weight to a height that equals its own length," Coll pursued desperately. "Not unless they are prepared to lift it through an arc from the point where its base will rest. And think what that would involve, Niall—raising one end of it to arm's length, first of all; then pushing that end higher with poles or maybe with the oars of their boats, until the whole length was finally upright and they could let it fall forward against the wall. And all the time they did this, having to steady it with ropes to keep it from slipping sideways!"

The Romans were beginning to form up in column of four, with the completed ladder resting on the shoulders of the men in the two middle ranks. Coll spared one glance for this latest development, and finished hastily,

"Just imagine, Niall, how open they would all lay themselves to our aim in the course of such a difficult exercise. Their commander would be a fool to try it!"

"Then he *is* a fool," Niall retorted, "for he *is* going to try it!"

One arm swept out to indicate the fourfold column now wheeling to face the Stronghold from a point on the far side of its entrance passage. Coll caught at the arm and yelled,

"But even if they do get it up, the whole thing will be so unstable it will be more dangerous to them than to us! It is a trick, Niall, only a trick to—"

The war cry of the Boar drowned the rest of his words, Domnall's voice leading the long, discordant howl. Niall wrenched himself free, all his former coolness submerged in sudden wild excitement; and raising his voice along with the rest, he rushed for the threatened part of the gallery's wall. Coll clutched at other figures scrambling to reach the same point, and found himself holding fast to the tunics of Finn and Becuma.

"You two!" he challenged. "You were told to stay on guard above the entrance passage, and I order you to obey. I order you to stay here with me."

"But, Coll—" they protested together. "But, Coll—" and stared resentfully down from their superior height. It flashed through Coll's mind that now, if ever, was the time to exercise the power that Taran had said could be his to command, and with bold determination he faced the mutiny in their stares.

"Remember that *I* am Master of the Stronghold," he told them sharply, "and you will do as I say or be forever barred from it."

They hesitated, throwing doubtful glances from him to one another, then Finn said sullenly, "But we are warriors, Coll. And all the fighting will be over there."

A nod of his head indicated the stamping, shouting mass of warriors facing the Roman advance, but Coll could see how his threat had weakened their first rebellion and he pressed the advantage home.

"No," he insisted. "It will be here, above the entrance passage; and *you* will have the glory of it!"

Finn and Becuma looked disbelieving, but they did not try to contradict him, and Coll threw a swift look in the direction of the Roman advance. The curve of the Stronghold's wall was beginning to hide this from him, but a scramble upward to stand on the parapet brought it once more fully into his view. They were still coming on in column of four, he saw then, trotting slowly with upraised shields interlocked against the javelins hurled intermittently from above. But all this was still just a blind —a diversion from the form the real attack would take!

Coll's eyes rested on the symmetrical pattern of the upraised shields. That attack, he realized, would come at the first hint of a break in their pattern, for the area around the Stronghold was too open to allow a force to steal secretly to the door. And it *would* be the door that was attacked again, for the Roman commander would certainly not risk losing half his men in a scaling attempt that was bound to fail. But he had not yet fully tested the door's defenses; and even though it was certain these could not be penetrated, he still should not be allowed the satisfaction of a successful diversion from his attempt to do so.

The trotting column quivered to a halt, but the shields remained firmly in position. "Be ready!" Coll snapped, and with an instant reflex of obedience, the other two crouched to grasp the boulders lining the parapet in front of them. As abruptly as smooth water shattered by a flung stone, the mass of interlocked shields showered apart, and the close Roman formation was suddenly a diffuse activity of figures darting into position for raising the ladder.

Except for one column of ten men peeling smartly off from the main group and drawing swords as they ran low and swiftly for the entrance passage!

Resolutely keeping his eyes from the diversion the main group was staging around the ladder, Coll judged the pace of this column. The leading man entered his firing line, and he yelled,

"*Now*, Finn!"

Finn heaved his boulder, but before it struck the first man and sent him spinning, Coll had yelled again and Becuma's boulder went hurtling down to land on the next man and send both him and the one who followed crashing earthward.

"*Rally! Niall, rally!*"

Swinging round to send his shout along the gallery, Coll left the other two to continue aiming at will, and glimpsed Niall's dismayed face surging toward him.

"How many into the entrance?" Niall reached him, gasping out the question, and it was Becuma who answered,

"Four—but we can pick them off as they run out again."

Coll peered down from the parapet. Immediately below him, the bodies of six men killed in the second attempt on the door lay sprawled among the huddle of boulders and bodies remaining from the first attempt. A further glance showed him the main Roman force resuming close formation around the ladder, but now facing away from the Stronghold. Then Nectan's voice came in a triumphant shout,

"They are moving off! Coll! Niall! They are retreating!"

And they were, Coll realized. Just as he had always calculated would happen, their commander had decided to search for easier prey, instead of wasting men against such a strong defense! But would they leave without knowing the fate of their comrades trapped inside the entrance passage?

Coll stared after the column of men moving away from the Stronghold, then from the corner of his eye became aware of figures dashing across the open ground below—the four trapped men making their break for freedom. The hissing sound of javelins in flight reached his ear, and suddenly the running figures were stumbling under a monstrous rain of the weapons. But miraculously, one of the figures escaped the javelins showering from the gallery, and as it gained the ranks of its comrades at last, Coll turned to jump down from the parapet.

A score of hands stretched eagerly out to help him descend. The hands supported him down to the floor of the gallery, and, crowded there by every man who could possibly struggle within touching distance, he was knocked breathless and deafened by thumps and shouts of congratulation. The voice of Becuma addressing the departing Romans rose in a derisive yell above the din:

"Run, Romans, run! Run with the curse of the Boar on you!"

"That is for *me* to pronounce!"

Domnall's voice sounded through the laughter raised by Becuma's jeering shout, and Coll turned to see the

Druid heaving himself onto the parapet. The laughter stilled. Domnall raised his arms. The huge voice trumpeted out his first words of cursing, and the anticipation in the gallery turned suddenly to looks of bewildered question. The Roman commander looked back toward the trumpeting voice, then he raised his stick to halt the retreating column, and comprehension dawned on Coll. Some others in the gallery had also understood, it seemed, and from somewhere among the mass of returning smiles around him, a voice exclaimed,

"No wonder they listen! *He is cursing them in their own language!*"

Coll stared up at Domnall, and although he could not understand a word of his cursing, the hair rose on the back of his neck at the sound of it; the sight of the white-clad figure towering defiantly on the parapet sent wild excitement churning through him.

It had been right, at first, to bid Domnall to silence; but Domnall was still the priest of battles, and now that victory was theirs, it was right also that he should stand there within javelin throw of the Romans and hurl the voice of the Boar after them. It was right that he should tower there, wearing the war face of Ernunnos, the three-headed one. The enemy must see and hear the victory of the Boar; they must depart with the curse of the Boar upon them. Custom demanded it, and in the tribe of the Boar, custom was all. . . .

Coll felt a bubble of sound begin rising in his throat; the war cry of the Boar rising, rising into a long howl of defiance. A deep-smoldering fire in his brain burst into sudden flame. The blood sang in his ears, his sight blurred, and he saw nothing of the javelin that struck

Domnall until the white-clad figure came crashing off the parapet with one hand clutching at the shaft of the Roman weapon and the point of it embedded in his neck.

The body seemed to take a long time to fall. And somewhere in that long, time-distorted moment that shock was imposing on Coll's senses, he heard voices that wailed,

"Domnall is dead! Domnall is dead!"

Then suddenly time clicked back into place again, and the fantasy of the slowly falling white figure and the wailing voices resolved into the reality of Domnall's body lying on the floor of the gallery, with Clodha rushing to kneel beside it, and Taran turning from the still figure to shout harshly,

"But Domnall is not the only one who can curse the Romans in their own tongue!"

With a swift leaping movement he was onto the parapet and bellowing more of the Latin words at the Romans. They had resumed their orderly retreat by this time, but at this renewed shouting from the parapet, their commander once again glanced backward.

"Ave! Ave!" Taran roared. *"Amicus Romae sum! Amicus Romae sum!"*

The Roman commander halted to stare up at him. Taran stood straddle-legged, pointing arrogantly with his sword from the Stronghold to the sea and the surrounding countryside, and with each of these gestures he hurled another of the Latin phrases toward the commander.

The man made as if to move away, then hesitated as Taran shouted again even louder, repeating the phrases he had already used, and swinging his sword with even more arrogant emphasis. The performance drew a mutter of admiration from the watchers in the gallery, and with a further thrill of triumph running through him, Coll yielded also to this admiration. Taran had succeeded brilliantly in taking over Domnall's role, he admitted to himself, and he certainly deserved to be the hero of the hour.

The Roman commander turned finally to follow his men. Taran swung around in a movement that was intended to bring him leaping back to the floor of the gallery; but even as his feet left the parapet, there was a flash of something bright and sharp—the point of a javelin that seemed to rise from the floor beside Domnall's body.

The rising point pierced Taran in mid-leap, driving deep into his body. And it was Clodha's hand on the shaft behind the flashing blade; Clodha's hand that thrust it fiercely into Taran's heart. And the voice screaming a curse as he fell was Clodha's voice.

Coll reached her side in time to see her backing, white-faced, from the roar of angry challenge that followed the killing. Taran lay at her feet, eyes wide open in the shock of his death moment, the shaft of the javelin protruding from his chest still quivering with the force of her thrust. Nectan seized her by the shoulders, half protecting her from the anger of the others, half threatening her himself as he shouted,

"Why did you kill him, why? He was a hero, Clodha!"

"He was a traitor!" Clodha snapped. "He was not cursing up there, as he pretended. He was betraying us to the Romans—look!"

Wrenching away from Nectan, she thrust toward the place where Domnall lay; and pushing close at her heels,

Coll was astonished to see the javelin gone from his neck and his wound still bleeding. Clodha knelt swiftly and took the bloodstained head in her lap.

"Look!" she challenged again. "You all thought Domnall was dead. Taran thought that too, and so he also thought he had the chance to play traitor. But *I* saw that the Roman javelin had not fatally wounded the old man, *I* did not trust Taran's posturing, and I knew Domnall could tell me the meaning of all those strange words. And so I drew the javelin from his neck and he did tell me what they meant—ask him now, and you will see!"

Nectan knelt to bring his face closer to the exhausted one lolling on Clodha's lap.

"Speak to us, Domnall," he urged. "Tell us what Taran shouted, up there on the parapet."

Domnall's eyes flickered open. "Traitor," he mumbled. "*Amicus Romae sum*—I am a friend of Rome. *Iuro Mithrae*—I swear by . . ."

The mumbling words trailed into silence. Domnall's eyes closed, and his face grew still.

"He has fainted." Clodha leaned forward as she spoke, and tore a strip from the wide sleeve of Domnall's robe. "And he *will* die if this bleeding is not stanched."

Quickly she began bandaging the wound in his neck, and continued, "But you have heard him say enough to let you know I am speaking the truth, and this is the rest of it. *I am a friend of Rome. I swear by the altar of Mithras*—"

"Mithras? Who is he?" The interruption came from several points in the ring of puzzled faces bent over Domnall, and Nectan glanced up to say quietly,

"Mithras is the god of the Roman soldiers. They

236

swear by him, and believe an oath taken in his name."

"*I swear by the altar of Mithras*," Clodha repeated, "*I can give this Stronghold to you. These people watch the sea. They do not watch the land. Sail out of sight. They will leave the Stronghold. Return overland, and attack by surprise. They will be at your mercy.*"

The bandaging was completed. Clodha began taking off her cloak to make a pillow for Domnall's head, and as her hands reached up to the fastening of it, she finished defiantly,

"Now you know the meaning of Taran's shouts. And so now you know why I rose with the javelin in my hand, and killed him."

"The very javelin that had wounded Domnall!" Nectan spoke wonderingly, his eyes on Clodha's pale and challenging face; then on impulse he reached out to clasp the hands still resting on the fastening of her cloak.

"You did right, Clodha," he told her warmly. "And I am proud of you."

"I am Anu's daughter," Clodha answered. "I did what she would have done." And without any change of expression, she finished taking off her cloak and began folding it.

Nectan rose to his feet, beckoning Coll and Niall to him as he rose. "Why?" he asked them. "Does either of you know why Taran should have been so treacherous?"

"Power," Coll told him. "The power he hoped to get from a bargain with the Romans." And staring at Clodha still kneeling beside Domnall, remembering the night he had realized she would never cease to suspect Taran until he was safely dead, he told Nectan of the argument Taran had put to him that day at the Stronghold.

"But I thought I had convinced him I would never consent to such a bargain," he finished, and looked from Clodha to the dead face on the gallery floor.

It was a strong face, he thought, as strong in death as it had been in life; a handsome, clever face, but still that of a man who had lived in two worlds and had never succeeded in belonging properly to either of them. A sadness touched him for the waste that Taran's life had been, and he could feel no anger when Nectan said dryly,

"Evidently you did convince him, Coll; and that was why he had to stake everything on this last slim chance of bargaining with the Romans on his own account."

"Was it such a slim chance?" Niall's pointing finger took all three to the parapet to watch the raiders' craft shooting back toward the waiting merchantmen. "We shall soon know, Nectan. The only cover for these ships lies west of here, in the rocky inlets north of our lookout headland. If they beat west from the bay—"

"They come here for easy conquests and many slaves," Nectan interrupted. "But already they have lost fifteen men and gained nothing, and so they must go east to other settlements that offer easier prey. Besides which, why should they take any notice of Taran? He was a stranger to them—one of us, an enemy. Why should they base their actions on anything *he* promised?"

"I can tell you why," Coll said. "They would have nothing to lose but time if matters did not live up to his promise, for their commander will not risk having more of his men killed in another attack on the Stronghold. But if they did manage to surprise us, they could kill us all. Then they would be free to examine the Stronghold, and I think they would seize on that chance."

"That is how I would see it if I were their commander," Niall agreed. "After all, they have never encountered such a defense before in the islands. Nor do they yet know whether they will meet with it in all our other settlements, and so they are bound to want to discover any possible weakness in it."

Nectan shrugged. "You reason soundly, both of you," he acknowledged. "You could be right."

The parapet was now lined with heads turned toward the departing ships, and the nearer the long raiding craft drew to the clumsy merchantmen, the louder grew the general argument on the eventual course they would set. A number of the men began laying wagers, some on "east," others on "west"; and when the raiders shot past the waiting merchantmen, there was a shout from the winning "west" faction.

Nectan withdrew from the parapet, a wry grin of admission on his face. "They say you cannot teach an old dog new tricks," he remarked. "Which is wise enough, for it seems you two were right, after all. And so, what now, Niall?"

"They will not waste time in launching this 'surprise' attack," Niall told him. "We stay here in safety till they do. And then we laugh to see it fail as the first one did, and leave the Stronghold only when we know it is finally safe to do so."

"No!" Coll spoke loudly, in sudden contradiction. "We can do better than that, Niall. We can use the surprise attack to destroy the Romans!"

"Destroy the Romans!" Nectan stared in astonishment. "Coll, are you—"

"If they fail completely against us," Coll interrupted,

"they *will* go east to the other settlements. And that means death or capture for many of those who helped us build our safe refuge."

"We can warn the others of their danger," Nectan told him. "We *will* warn them!"

"But if we destroy the Romans," Coll persisted, "instead of simply fighting them off as we did the first time, we will banish that danger altogether from the islands— for this summer at least. And surely that is the better course."

"You talk like a fool," Nectan said sharply. "How can we do such a thing?"

Coll turned abruptly to Niall. "How much faith have you in this Stronghold?" he demanded. "Do you believe we could hold it, even if the door was breached?"

"Do *you* believe we can?" Niall countered.

"I know we can." Coll looked meaningfully at him. "I know that as certainly as I knew the Romans could never raise their ladder against it."

Niall flushed. "You have me there," he admitted. "Tell me anything about the Stronghold, Coll; anything at all, and I shall believe it."

"You are certain of that?"

"As certain as I am of tomorrow's sunrise."

"Then do you remember what Taran said about the Stronghold—that the perfect defense which fails becomes the perfect trap?"

"Taran is dead," Nectan began, but smoothly Coll interrupted again,

"—And has now paid all his debts to us with that very remark about the Stronghold. For this is what we will do. We will allow it to become a trap—but not for us. For the Romans!"

13

End and Beginning

The trap was set; and in the top gallery, where he had held a final conference with Coll, Niall prepared for his part in it.

Clodha was there to help with this, for since Domnall was too weak to be moved, it had been decided she would stay with him until the attack was over. Finn and Becuma were present also, acting as lookouts, and they threw grinning glances at one another as Clodha skillfully wove Niall's hair into a woman's braids. A woman's full-length dress over his own short tunic, and a bundle contrived to look like a sleeping baby strapped on his back, completed the transformation from warrior to woman; and presenting himself for inspection, he asked,

"Well? How do I look?"

"From the back view," Finn said critically, "a fine figure of a woman!"

There was a general laugh at this, but Niall had the last word. "That is the only view the Romans will have," he retorted; then, joining Coll at the parapet, he nodded down toward the settlement.

"And how does that look?" he asked. "Will that deceive the Romans?"

Coll studied the scene below. There was plenty of domestic to-ing and fro-ing among the houses now, he noted. The doorways held the figures of women bent to the quern and industriously grinding corn. More women had gathered at the stream to gossip and wash clothes. And far out among the rocks edging the beach, the men of the settlement were engaged in a variety of fishing tasks.

It looked, he thought, exactly as the Romans would expect to find it if the men had been deceived into leaving the Stronghold and permitting their womenfolk to take up normal life again. But, as in Niall's case, the plaited hair and long dress of every "woman" there disguised a warrior form. And the "men," apparently working too far away to reach them in time to stave off an attack, were simply the bodies of the dead Roman soldiers dressed in island costume and propped up into various suitable poses.

Coll looked up to nod toward the point at which the Romans would have to sweep over the ridge in order to achieve the necessary surprise in their attack.

"From there," he said, "it most certainly will deceive them. And if you remember to scream like women as you run for the Stronghold, that will help to keep up the deception."

"I will tell Nectan that," Niall remarked, and flashing a look at him, Coll saw the grin that accompanied the words. The thought of Nectan pitching his deep voice to a woman's scream touched an answering chord of amusement in himself, and for a moment, the whole serious business of preparing for the Romans seemed no more than just another of the escapades in the boyhood he and Niall had shared.

But only for a moment! Coll sobered, remembering that Niall would be the last man into the Stronghold when the attack finally came, and turned away to let him take his farewell of Clodha. Their whispered words came faintly to him; Clodha first, repeating the warning instruction Nectan had given Niall:

"*Remember they will come at you two at a time—the first one boring in to knock you off balance, the second one to strike at you.* Watch the second man!"

Niall's voice then—"*I have worked out how to counter that, Clodha, I promise you. . . .*"

There was a moment's silence, then Coll felt a brief, firm clasp on his shoulder, and Niall was gone, running lightly down through the galleries to join the other men in the settlement.

Coll moved to inspect the firebox full of smoldering torches, and the huge pile of oil-soaked hay filling the gallery at the point above the entrance to the Stronghold. Then, staring westward at the sun's lengthening rays, he wondered how much longer they would have before the attack.

Not long, he decided. The Romans would not have needed to sail very far before the massive cliffs of the west coast shut them out of sight. Voices sounding faintly from below brought his attention back to the settlement; and with satisfaction he saw Echu the smith herding some milk cows toward the Stronghold, and Niall marshaling the rest of his force in imitation of the women's usual evening procession to draw water from the stream.

That was good, he thought approvingly. They were managing to have every man positioned so that their whole force now had the advantage of being placed between the Stronghold and the Romans' appearance on the ridge. A low murmur of laughter came from farther along the gallery, where Finn and Becuma were standing; and moving toward them, Coll saw them grinning down on the sight of their disguised companions.

"Finn!" he called sharply. "Those men down there are depending on you for the first warning. Keep your eyes on the land beyond the ridge. And you, Becuma, remember there is always a faint chance they might still decide on another attack from the sea. Keep your eyes on the bay."

Guiltily, Finn and Becuma hastened to obey, and stillness took over in the gallery. Coll turned to glance down at Domnall lying with his head pillowed on Clodha's cloak, his face almost as white as the linen around his neck. Clodha, kneeling patiently at the old man's head, looked up to meet the question in Coll's eyes, and said quietly,

"He will live—at least until I can gather the proper herbs for dressing his wound. And then he will quickly recover."

If he himself lived to be a hundred, Coll thought, he would never understand Clodha! To be capable of killing a strong young man in one breath, yet to turn in the next breath and give devoted nursing to a sick old man—this was surely all part of what it meant to be the girl who would one day become Mother of the Boar. But how could any man—or for that matter of it, how could any ordinary woman—ever understand a nature that was at once so fierce and so compassionate?

Clodha leaned over to dab sweat off the pale face upturned to her. The stiff lips moved, muttering incomprehensibly. The veined eyelids fluttered, then opened slowly, like those of a corpse rolling open. Slate-gray eyes stared vacantly up at Coll, then seemed to focus on him. The dry lips shaped a sound.

"You—you are—"

Coll bent to hear the whispering voice, and with faintly returning strength, it continued hoarsely,

"You are—young. Why are you not—down there . . . with them . . . ? Other young men—fighting . . . fighting Romans. . . ."

Coll glanced doubtfully at Clodha. She nodded an indication that he should answer, and patiently he explained,

"It is part of our plan that all the men down there must be able to run fast—faster than the Romans. And I am a cripple. Had you forgotten?"

"Cripple . . . ?" Domnall repeated the word vacantly, and then signed. "Ah, yes, I remember—Bran's brother."

To Coll's dismay, then, the slate-gray stare was suddenly brilliant with tears. The veined eyelids drooped, spilling the teardrops in trickles down the grooves of the tired old face, and Domnall mumbled,

"Bran . . . I loved him. He was my son, the child of my heart. And I killed him. . . ."

Coll straightened and, with a helpless shrug toward Clodha was about to turn away, but the Druid's eyes snapped suddenly open again. Their gaze focused once more on him; and still speaking slowly, but clearly now, Domnall continued,

"Bran had a gentle nature. And you have some of that same gentleness in yours. But you also have a core of iron in you that Bran never had. Coll, brother of my heart's son, you will win this battle!"

The eyes closed, dismissing any reply to this pronouncement even before Coll's startled understanding had grasped it; and leaning over the parapet again, he thought what an odd conversation it had been. And yet he could feel himself strangely moved by it—almost as if he were beginning to like this terrible, extraordinary old man!

With smiling wonder he considered this idea, then, putting it aside for future examination, concentrated his attention on the men marshaled beside the stream.

They were still disposed in the attitudes Niall had dictated; some kneeling to dip water jars in the stream, others gathered in the little gossiping groups it was the women's habit to form. But there was no gossiping in these groups!

Silent, unmoving, they stood with eyes fixed on the Stronghold, patiently waiting for the first signal Finn would give. The kneeling "women," bent perpetually to the stream as if frozen in position, were silent also. Only the stream itself talked, as it rippled brightly over the stones. Only Echu's little herd of cows moved restlessly, easing the discomfort of full udders straining to be milked. . . .

A scouting party trotting briskly toward the ridge gave the first warning of the Romans' appearance. Finn made the prearranged signal of letting a boulder drop from the parapet, and as it touched the ground the groups beside the stream broke into a flurry of simulated activity.

Crouching down so that he could just see above the parapet then, and motioning Finn and Becuma to keep down altogether, Coll watched the scouts' advance become more and more cautious, until eventually they were crawling to reach the top of the ridge. For several minutes they lay there, their heads turning from the "men" isolated far out on the beach, to the "women" making play of drawing water and gossiping beside the stream.

Coll ducked before the turning heads could be raised to study the Stronghold. Faintly, from below, he heard the cattle bellowing, and knew that Echu must now be driving them leisurely into the central courtyard, as if to pen them there for the evening milking. Eyes closed, he tried to visualize the scouts reporting to their commander.

. . . All back to normal . . . womenfolk returned . . . men fishing . . . no guards posted . . . Stronghold no more than a cattle pen now . . . place an easy mark. . . .

Surely that was what they would say? Men were never suspicious, after all, of what they *expected* to see, and the appearance of the settlement now was exactly what Taran had led the Romans to expect.

Opening his eyes again, Coll wondered if it was time for another look over the parapet. The scouts would not risk staying for very long, he decided and, half straightening himself, peered warily downward. There was no sign now of the scouts watching from the ridge, and a few moments later he saw figures that rose from a crawling position to begin a purposeful trot in a northwesterly direction.

"Second signal, Finn," he said quietly; and rising, Finn let another stone drop from the parapet.

The pretense of activity below subsided into a further waiting stillness. The noise of the cattle in the courtyard rose louder as Echu began driving them back to the open. They broke out from the entrance and, bellowing still more plaintively, headed back to the settlement and their accustomed stalls. Echu joined one of the groups by the stream. Finn stood ready to drop the boulder that would be his final signal. . . .

Somehow Coll had not expected his reaction to the eventual return of the main Roman force. He was still not afraid of them, he realized. He never would be afraid of them again! Calmly he watched the advancing column of soldiers reach the point where they would deploy into position for sweeping over the ridge.

"I will time this signal also," he told Finn. "And Becuma, start blowing up the torches."

Becuma seized a hand bellows and furiously pumped flame out of the torches smoldering in their firebox. The Roman commander raised his stick, and the marching column of soldiers deployed into open order. Bending low, they charged toward the ridge; and in the second before they appeared in silhouette on its crest, Coll spoke quietly and Finn dropped his boulder.

In a surging wall of shields that covered them from chest to ankle, their short Roman swords held in a rigid, bent-elbowed grip, the soldiers swept down from the ridge. The "women" waiting tensely by the stream broke into screaming, panicked flight to the Stronghold; and as they ran, Becuma thrust two of the flaming torches into the hay piled against the parapet.

Coll leaned over the parapet, coolly timing his next move. The tall yellow-haired "woman" was Niall, and Niall would be the last into the Stronghold. . . .

Niall reached the entrance with only a couple of spears' lengths between him and the first of the pursuing soldiers. The torch flames were licking up through the hay now. Becuma and Finn had snatched up pitchforks. Coll swung round and darted to the parapet of the gallery's inner wall. Niall had gained as far as the entrance to the stairway, and armed with the sword and shield planted in readiness for him, was turning at bay there.

The first two soldiers came at him, as Nectan had warned, with the tactics that placed their own long shields and short swords to the greatest advantage over Niall's long sword and small shield. Crouching, the leading man angled his shield to protect both himself and the left flank of the second man, and bore down on Niall's right, with the intention of blocking his sword arm and knocking him off balance to a frontal stab from the second man.

Niall countered with a jumping kick that landed flat-footed against the shield of the man on his right. The soldier staggered back, his shield flying aside to expose the second man's left flank.

But Niall's jump meant that his own left side was exposed, and as his feet touched ground again, the second man angled himself to thrust at it. Niall's recovery became a pivoting movement, with his shield flashing down to intercept the short, stabbing blade, and his own long sword swinging to arc downward across the buttocks of the second man.

It was all over in seconds, but even so, there was now

another handful of soldiers surging across the central courtyard. Niall leaped for the stairs, and a muffled thunder of rock falling told Coll that he had gained the head of the first flight in time to allow the loosing of the avalanche of stone that would block it to the Romans.

The hay was beginning to blaze, and the first of their own men to reach the top gallery were snatching up the weapons laid ready for them. Coll furiously signaled to them to keep down out of sight, and then looked cautiously down from the outer parapet.

About a third of the Romans, he estimated, were now either inside the Stronghold or running down the entrance passage; and these men had not yet realized they were trapped, for their commander was still motioning others inside. But he had formed at least half of his men into a guard outside the entrance; and clearly, from the direction of his gaze, he was now suspicious of the immobility of the "men" out at the rocks.

Coll drew his head back sharply. His gaze sweeping the gallery saw that the greater part of their own force was now there, with Nectan among those crouched behind the inner parapet. Silently he signaled Finn and Becuma, and lifting a mass of the blazing hay on their pitchforks, they dropped it straight down on the guard at the mouth of the entrance passage.

"*Now!*" Coll yelled as it fell; and the word exploding from him brought every man in the gallery to his feet, with weapons at the ready.

The javelins of those at the outer parapet shot down on the soldiers running out from under the fiery descent of the hay. But the Romans were quick to protect themselves, and quick to realize how the fire now blocking the entrance would trap those of their comrades already inside the Stronghold.

With their shields held over their heads they crowded back to the fire, poking at the hay with their swords in an effort to disperse it; and yelling again to make himself heard above the growing noise of battle, Coll ordered,

"Use stones! Smash those shields down!"

Exultantly, the Men of the Boar obeyed, and boulder after boulder hurtled down to smash on a shield with a force that sent the soldier underneath it crashing to earth. Finn and Becuma sent another load of fire down; and as they jabbed their pitchforks into the remainder of the hay, Niall arrived at Coll's elbow.

Panting from his rush up the stairs, he leaned over to review the position at the entrance; and leaving him to continue in command at that side of the gallery, Coll darted to Nectan's position at the inner parapet.

Nectan was holding his men back until he judged that the second load of fire had created enough smoke in the entrance passage to drive out any Roman hiding there. Coll peered over the inner parapet to see one soldier come stumbling out; and, still coughing and spluttering from the smoke, stand staring at the rest of his trapped comrades now waiting close in to the foot of the walls with their shields held above their heads.

"All together now!" Nectan roared, and with an astonished jerk of his head toward the sound, the soldier ran for cover.

But there was no cover, Coll thought grimly. With the entrance passage full of smoke, all the guard cells blocked up, and the entrance to the stairway full of rock, there was nowhere the soldier could hide from the death hurtling down from the top gallery and from the window opening of every gallery beneath it. Nowhere any of the Romans could hide!

Nor was there any mercy among the Men of the Boar, for every one of them had some memory, however distant, of a raid that had meant one of their own blood kin killed or captured by Roman soldiers; and every stone that smashed down a shield, every javelin that pierced the body rolling from beneath its cover, was revenge for the bitterness of those memories. With voices soaring in response to Nectan's roars of encouragement, they aimed and threw with unrelenting ferocity; and gazing down on the scattered shields, the sprawling bodies, and the blood that patchily reddened the trampled earthen floor of the courtyard, Coll was coldly aware of his own revenge.

Rome had crippled him; but Rome, he told himself, was *not* all-powerful. Domnall had said that, and now *he* had proved it. The thought of Domnall impelled him to turn and begin working a way through the wild activity in the gallery. Domnall would want to see this final destruction of the Romans, he decided. Domnall *should* see it—if he still lived, and had not been trampled underfoot in all this turmoil!

Determinedly Coll moved to the spot where Domnall had been laid, only to find that the old man was already on his feet, supported half by his own grip on the parapet, and half by Clodha's strong young arms. And he was cursing the Romans! The great voice was reduced to a whisper, but there was still no mistaking the intent of those moving lips, for the vengefulness in Domnall's face gave clear evidence of their message.

With a sense of awe at the will that had brought him to his feet, Coll moved to the outer parapet. The commotion there was now being caused by men grappling ropes to it; and leaning over to watch the ropes dropping down on the outside of the wall, he saw all that were left of the Romans—a mere sixteen or so—beginning their retreat from the Stronghold.

Niall was first over the parapet in the slide downward to pursue them; and as the outer parapet cleared of men, the men at the inner parapet and those in the galleries below turned from their completed slaughter and surged to join the pursuit. The Romans turned at bay: desperate men, with no hope of reaching the advantage of higher ground ahead of the fleet-footed islanders, and no other defensive position possible on the open space between them and the ridge.

Coll saw that their commander was wounded. But he still had the strength to lift his stick for the order that drew his men up in close formation. He still had the courage to place himself at their head and face the enemy with his sword at the ready.

Coll did not wait to see the blow that struck him down. The Romans had paid their debts to him, he thought. His Stronghold had proved itself. The rest of the islands were safe for one more summer, and he did not want to see a brave man die. Mentally saluting the doomed commander and his men, he turned back toward Clodha and Domnall, and the debris of battle in the gallery.

They worked, all of them, with little sleep that night, to dispose of the bodies; for Nectan had ordered that this must be done before the women could be allowed to return.

Coll and Clodha between them had managed to lower Domnall gently from the parapet before sliding down themselves. But in accordance with the rule that forbade his entering under a family roof, he had to be made comfortable in a shelter contrived against the defensive wall of the dun; and this was where Anu found him the following day when Nectan's messengers had summoned back her and her charges.

Coll did not see that meeting, since he was too busy directing the restoration of his Stronghold to its original defensive state. But he heard from Clodha of the dispute between the two of them over the correct choice of herbs for dressing Domnall's wound, and of the outcome of that dispute.

"Domnall," said Clodha maliciously, "knows everything about everything—or so he thinks! But when he tried to lay down the law over the healing property of this herb and that herb, he forgot that no one except Anu rules in Anu's dun!"

Coll grinned at her tone. "Nevertheless," he remarked, "he is a learned man, Clodha, and there are a few questions I would like to ask him."

With the questions still in his mind on the second day after the victory of the Stronghold, he noted the litter being prepared to carry Domnall back to the Ring, and made an opportunity to speak to him before he left.

"I found these where some of the Romans fell," he said hesitantly, and showed Domnall a handful of coins. "Can you tell me what they are?"

"*Denarii*," Domnall answered promptly. "The pay of the soldiers."

"Pay?" Coll questioned.

"Yes—money, coins," Domnall told him. "A Roman soldier is given these in return for fighting. He buys food with them, or clothes, or anything else he needs. That is their system."

It sounded a foolish system to Coll. For why should a man be paid coins for courage, instead of the respect of his fellow men? And how, in any case, could the value of a coin be judged against that of a fur, or a piece of cloth, or a dish of meat?

Domnall listened without comment as he expressed these views, then seized on the next object of Coll's questions.

"Now this," he remarked, "is of greater interest! This is an amulet of Mithras, the god of the Roman soldiers. Keep this, Coll. It is always useful to know something of the faith of your enemies."

Domnall's voice had regained some of its normal strength, and listening to him, it occurred to Coll that he was recovering fast—and in more ways than one. He grinned inwardly at the thought, then was sobered by the remembrance of his next question. With a flush mounting to his face, he forced himself to form it into words.

"I would also like to know if— Have you forgiven me?"

The face looking up at him grew still as stone—carven, unforgiving stone. Then, to his unbounded relief, Domnall said quietly,

"How can I withhold forgiveness so well deserved and

so truly earned? You need not ask for what is already yours."

"And when you named Fand for sacrifice, was it indeed because you believed the gods had ruled so?"

He had not meant to ask that last question, Coll realized. It simply seemed to have come blurting out from him without warning, and even as he heard his own voice he was aghast at himself. But the carved appearance of Domnall's face was not altering by so much as the twitch of a muscle, and his voice was still quiet as he said,

"I live close with the gods, but even I cannot always know their will. My duty is therefore a difficult one, but I must still try to do it for the good of all, and thus I have always tried."

There was no answer to that, Coll thought—no answer except argument, for Domnall's words could be taken to mean anything anyone wanted them to mean. But he did not want to argue with Domnall. There had been more than enough of that already!

The Druid spoke again, breaking the silence that had fallen.

"Be always grateful that Bran freely gave his life for that of Fand, and for your right to build the Stronghold. It was a cruel exchange; cruel for him—and for me."

"No man could ever forget a brother such as Bran," Coll assured him gravely. "He will always be in my mind, as much as he is in yours."

Domnall's slate-gray stare held his, probing, seeking the truth. And somehow finding it without a word spoken, Coll thought; and turned away at last feeling it would take more than one lifetime to understand this strange, powerful old man. Yet Bran had understood him enough to love him—but Bran, of course, had been different from ordinary people. . . .

When the litter was eventually ready, and Domnall had been installed in it, he joined the crowd milling around its bearers. Domnall beckoned to him, and said when he approached,

"I have told you that you are a discoverer. You are one of those who can think; and now I shall tell you what this means. You are one of those the gods have gifted with the nature to seek that for which the Druids—alone among the priests of all faiths—perpetually seek: the secret source of life itself. Be grateful for this also; for in the seeking you will discover the nature also of your fellow man, and thus gain knowledge which is more than mere happiness."

One veined, powerful hand came down to rest briefly on Coll's head; then imperiously it signaled to the litter bearers to move off. Coll stared after the litter with Domnall's words echoing in his mind—*the secret source of life itself.* So that was the aim that had engrossed the whole of Bran's short life! That was the reason for all the mathematics, the poetry, the magic—and finally the meaning behind the old hand driving the bronze knife, and the young body spurting blood to the rising sun. . . .

"Coll, you have work to do!"

Nectan's voice brought him back to the present moment, and guiltily he faced about to the scores of eyes watching him.

"The other settlements must be taught how to build their own Strongholds," Nectan continued briskly, "and we have experienced men here who can go with you to help them. Pick those who will be of most use to you,

Coll. Form your team with them, and start off."

"Straightaway? Today?" Coll asked.

"Why not? There will be no more raids this summer, but the sooner you start, the farther you can spread your teaching before next summer comes."

"He cannot start straightaway!" The protesting voice was Fand's; and catching her eye as she came to stand by him, Coll smiled and agreed,

"No. Not straightaway, Nectan. Fand will be coming with me, and so first we must be married."

"A younger daughter cannot be married before an older one," Niall pointed out, and drew Clodha toward him. "Is the Boar ready for its new Chief, Nectan?"

Nectan glanced at Conamaill, and found the elderly face smiling. Anu was smiling also, and with a shrug that accepted this verdict, he looked from her face to the expectant faces of the four young people.

"Very well," he agreed. "I make this my last decree as Chief of the Boar. Let there be marriages first, and *then* let there be building!"

And more building, and more building; and more and more, until there were Strongholds wherever a man looked on the islands! And perhaps on the mainland too, where other tribes ran every summer from the raiders ...! Somewhere beyond the rejoicing faces all around him, Coll saw his dream of the Stronghold enlarged to a vision of coastline after coastline dominated by towering, impregnable defenses; defenses strong enough to stand for generation upon generation, until Rome was finally defeated and there was no further need of his Strongholds.

But even then they would still stand for a wonder and a sign of those who had lived long ago. The dream would last. Those who came after would be aware it had once been. . . .

Fand's fingers, slipped into his own, brought Coll's mind back to earth. And briskly, keeping tight hold of the hand he had won, he began selecting the men who would labor with him to realize the dream.